Faith, Lies, and the Opinion Polls

Faith, Lies, and the Opinion Polls

WILLIAM H. HINSON
with Carole Sanderson Streeter

*If everybody's doin' it,
it ain't worth much!*

VICTOR BOOKS

A DIVISION OF SCRIPTURE PRESS PUBLICATIONS INC.
USA CANADA ENGLAND

Scripture quotations are from the *Holy Bible: New International Version*®.
Copyright © 1973, 1978, 1984 by International Bible Society. Used by
permission of Zondervan Publishing House. All rights reserved.

Editor: James R. Adair
Cover Designer: Joe DeLeon

Library of Congress Cataloging-in-Publication Data

Hinson, William H., 1936-
    Faith, lies, and the opinion polls / by William H. Hinson; with Carole
Sanderson Streeter.
        p. cm.
    ISBN 1-56476-123-1
    1. Christian life—Methodist authors.   I. Streeter, Carole Sanderson.
II. Title.
BV4501.2.H5214   1993
248.4—dc20   93-13694
                                                                           CIP

© 1993 by SP Publications, Inc. All rights reserved.
Printed in the United States of America.

1 2 3 4 5 6 7 8 9 10 Printing/Year 97 96 95 94 93

To our children:
Elizabeth Hinson Elder
John Laird Hinson
Catherine Hinson Hicks
whose lives fill us with inestimable joy and pride.

Contents

Introduction

Drayton McLane, Jr., a millionaire businessman from Temple, Texas, purchased the Houston Astros baseball team in the fall of 1992. At the first press conference following the purchase, Mr. McLane was subjected to a barrage of questions from sports writers. They were interested in whether or not he was going to go after some big-name, high-priced free agents in baseball. Houston is hungry for a pennant, and the sports writers wanted to know how the new owner was going to turn the Astros into pennant contenders.

Drayton McLane answered the reporters' questions patiently. And interspersed with talk about shortstops, pitchers, and free agents, McLane, a devout Christian, stated his intention to run the Astros ball club according to Christian principles.

When the press conference concluded, one reporter lingered. As the new owner was leaving the pressroom, the reporter asked him about his comments. "Mr. McLane, I understand about shortstops, outfielders, and free agents, but I'm puzzled. What do Christian principles have to do with baseball?"

According to the 1990 census, 137 million people in the United States are adherents of organized religion. That is 55.1 percent of the population. In polls that followed up on the census, gathering more specific information on the practices of these religious people, the same kind of question appeared as that posed by the reporter to Drayton McLane. What *do* Christian principles and beliefs have to do with the real world?

There is a wide chasm between the beliefs and the behavior of professing Christians. Studies beyond the recent polls have borne out the conclusion that those who claim to be Christians often behave in almost the same way as those who do not.

Have we become a nation of schizophrenics? Holding what we call belief in one part of our being, and then shaping our behavior in another part, and keeping the two separate?

What indeed do Christian principles have to do with baseball and the rest of the real world?

CHAPTER

One

I Can Hear You Clucking, but I Can't Find Your Nest

According to the 1990 census, 137 million people in the United States are adherents of organized religion. That is 55.1 percent of the population. But the Gallup Poll samplings that followed up this census gathered more detailed information about the specific religious beliefs and practices of these people, and especially of those who professed to follow Jesus Christ.

It is good news that so many people go to church. But it is very bad news that there is virtually no difference in the day-to-day behavior of those who claim to be Christians and those who do not.

Great numbers of professing Christians and secularists alike are without moral leadership. Ninety percent of us claim that we believe in God, but the overwhelming majority of people—93 percent!—say that they and nobody else determine what is and what isn't moral in their lives. They base their decisions on their own experience. When they want to answer a question of right and wrong, they ask themselves.

Almost as large a majority—84 percent—confess that they would violate the established rules of their religion if they thought the rules were wrong. Christians as well as secularists seem to have become a law unto themselves.

Better than 55 percent of the American people belong to a church, but surveys reveal that the rules that many people actually live by are very different from the commandments they hear in church. Researchers James Patterson and Peter Kim in *The Day America Told the Truth* say that 77 percent of us don't see the point in observing the Lord's Day; 74 percent indicate that they think it is all right to steal from those who will not really miss it; 64 percent feel it is okay to lie so long as it does not cause any real damage; 53 percent acknowledge that they would cheat on their spouse, and also believe that given the chance, the spouse would do the same.

Christians are not very different from non-Christians in terms of the authority issue. The George Barna research group discovered that there are almost as many professing Christians as non-Christians who strongly agree that "there is no such thing as absolute truth." Almost 75 percent of the Baby Busters, those born after 1965, agree that there is no absolute truth. Even among the elderly of our land, 56 percent do not believe that there is any such thing as absolute truth.

At the heart of our Christian faith is the belief that God sent His only Son, Jesus, into the world to save us from our sins. Barna's research reveals, however, that 83 percent of adults contend that people are basically good. Amazingly, people professing to be born-again Christians also buy into this notion. A strong majority of professing believers—77 percent—accept the idea that people are basically good. For those who hold such views, Christmas and Easter are enjoyable festivals which enhance their lives, but what they celebrate is not really related to their salvation.

Situation Ethics

We are all a mix of dust and divinity, and this is at once a part of our greatness and also a part of our challenge. The Bible says that God knows we are but dust, and it also offers us the possibility of living with Christ in resurrection power. God understands our sin and weakness, but He also offers a higher way to live. There is a standard, a better way. And yet, so often the lower part of ourselves, the dust, if you please, seems to win over the spirit. Why this happens is a complex matter that has to do with our human nature.

When I was in seminary, Joseph Fletcher published his book *Situation Ethics* and it was a bombshell. Even now, thirty-two years later, we are still living in the fallout of that book. Fletcher was a pioneer in the field of medical ethics and taught for a long time in a seminary. He advanced the idea that we are to be guided in any situation by asking ourselves, "What is the loving thing to do?"

Fletcher believed there were no absolutes and that every situation must be judged on its own merits. He did not take into account our lower nature, our dust. He didn't admit that our consideration of "the loving thing" would quite naturally lead us to what we wanted and loved to do. It was a small step to a popular philosophy of the '90s: "Do your own thing. If it feels right for you, it is right. What is right for me may not be for you, but that is fine, because there is no absolute standard."

For Fletcher, the holy estate of marriage became a social

custom and convenience. And because so many people in our culture have bought into this mentality, we listen to a professional athlete boast about sleeping with 2,500 women, or a young man from a famous family getting massive media attention while he is being tried for rape. Both of these men were treated as minor heroes whose words were spread across the land as if they were truth. They followed Joseph Fletcher and went for it all. They did their own thing.

In contrast, I want to tell you about another young man, John, who had a beautiful wife and several small children. He also was doing well in his professional life.

Yet, John was in distress when he came to talk with me, because he knew that his feelings were not going to be adequate anymore to make his marriage work. If you are married, you know what I mean. After three years or ten years, every married couple finally comes to this point. Without commitment, the feelings are not going to suffice.

John's wife, Linda, was worn out from chasing after their children all day. Their finances were tight, and they could not go out like they used to or take the vacations they wanted. He was working hard all day, and often felt unloved and unappreciated. And Linda felt the same way.

Into this vulnerable situation came another person—a single woman in John's office who was very attractive. She sent him signals that she was lonely and that she understood him and thought he was wonderful. They began to talk and to spend more and more time together. There are people who believe that talking is the most intimate human activity. And John began to share his intimate thoughts with her in a way he had not done with his frazzled wife for a long time.

By the time he made the appointment with me, John was committing emotional adultery with this woman, and he knew that if the relationship continued much longer, his marriage would soon be over. He would be involved in an extramarital affair.

John and I prayed about this problem, and God got through to him that day so that he remembered who he was and what he was—dust, yes, but also a child of God.

When he went back to work, he called the young woman into his office and said to her, "You are an attractive and fine person. If I were living in another life, we could probably be sweethearts and maybe even marry. But I want you to know that I have made a commitment to my wife and my marriage, and this commitment is until death parts us. I pledged my fidelity, and I will never, ever break that vow and that commitment."

The story has a happy ending. Not only did John and Linda's marriage survive and prosper in beautiful ways, but the young woman became a Christian because of John's witness. She could receive what he said about his faith because she saw him making a difficult decision to do what was right.

Telltales in the Cathedral

When my wife, Jean, and I were in England a few years ago, we visited the city of York where we toured Yorkminster, a historic and glorious cathedral. We were told that in 1967, some cracks appeared in the stonework of the great edifice. The engineers who were called in knew they had to determine if the building was indeed shifting. The way they did this was to take some small pieces of glass called "telltales" and glue them across the cracks in the cathedral. On the first day when they checked the telltales, they found three of them broken, a sure indication that the whole structure was in danger because of a shifting foundation. The next step was to fix the foundation, a process that was so major and took so many tons of concrete that the cathedral charged admission for visitors to see what the engineers were doing.

Jesus told a story about two buildings. One of them had a good foundation and the other did not. The wise man had built his house on the rock and the foolish man on the sand. The test came for both when the storms began, the streams rose, and the winds blew and beat against the houses. One of them was left standing, but the other fell with a great crash (Matt. 7:24-27).

Jesus said that everyone who put His words into practice was like the wise man. Even in His time, there were people who professed one thing and did another, and so He made it clear that mere profession of discipleship was not adequate. There had to be something to back it up. People were good at saying "Lord, Lord" in pious tones, but that did not mean they were going to enter the kingdom of heaven. Only those who do the will of the Father are part of the kingdom.

I Can Hear You Clucking . . .

This test of Christian character reminds me of a clucking hen on our farm when I was a boy. My mother had an ear for the clucking hens. She knew that no matter how well she prepared the hens' nests on the side of the barn or behind the garage, invariably a few chickens would go out to a field or the edge of the forest to nest. They wanted to hide their eggs. The only answer was to follow the clucking hen to her nest.

You can imagine my impatience on a sunny afternoon when I wanted to do something I enjoyed, only to have my mother say, "A chicken is clucking. I want you to follow her to her nest." And so I'd spend my afternoon waiting for a silly clucking chicken to lead me to her nest.

The most disgusting experience I had as a young boy was to follow a chicken all afternoon, only to see her at last go to the roost with the rest of them, and to realize that there was no nest full of eggs. She clucked when she had nothing to cluck about.

This makes me think of so many people in our society today who cluck and claim that they are Christians, but who don't live any differently than the rest of the world. Jesus said that we will know His disciples by the fruit that they produce. But these people have no more spiritual fruit than my clucking chicken had eggs.

Jesus warned that some of these people might even be false prophets. He called them wolves in sheep's clothing, because they seemed for all the world like real prophets. When they appeared in Moses' day, he gave orders to stone them. Jeremiah lamented that the false prophets of his day had brought their licentious and self-centered ways into the temple of God.

The New Testament church was not free of false prophets, anymore than we are today. Paul told the Corinthian church to pray for a spirit of discernment to determine who was a true or false prophet. These preachers were so plausible with their arguments. They always made Christianity sound easier than it is. It was necessary to apply the test, not of doctrine but of behavior. Jesus said we would know the true believers by the quality of their lives. The proof is in the practice.

Clucking Christians and Evangelism
When Jean and I were in England, we visited the city of Plymouth from which the Pilgrims sailed to come to the New World in 1620. As I stood on the spot from which the *Mayflower* left, I thought of the pastor who went with them, John Robinson. Before they sailed, he charged the people in these words, "I charge you to follow me only as far as you see me following Jesus Christ. Follow me only that far."

What he told the Pilgrims is what we have to say to our

world. People who profess one thing but do another cause great harm to the church of Christ. If we wonder why the church is not making more impact in our society, if we wonder why primitive religions are encroaching in lands that once were Christian, we need to look to the fruit production in Christians, the quality of Christian character, the degree of likeness to the Spirit of God.

When the Apostle Paul wrote to the early church, he said, "Remember what you have seen and heard and received from me and the God of peace will be with you." In Paul's day the Good News was spread by word of mouth, since no Gospels were yet written. Paul and the other apostles were carrying the Word of God in their stories and in their lives. And so Paul said, "Remember what you have seen in me." The people who live and work near you, who never go to church, read only one Bible—you. If your witness is not compelling, you need to take a look at your profession and also at your practice of faith.

Ask yourself if you are doing a lot of clucking without having anything to cluck about. One reason more people do not receive Christ as Savior is that they are trying to find the nest. They want to see the proof.

There is no place to hide from the call to obedience. We are all building a house that is very obvious to other people. We are building brick by brick, and we have to live in those houses now, and then they will follow us right on into eternity.

While two houses may look almost alike, and while the same storm may hit the houses, the response to the storm will tell the story. Your life may seem almost like that of many people you know. But when the storm comes, as it will, then you—and others—will know the strength of your spiritual foundation.

An amateur had paid big bucks to enter a pro-am tournament in Memphis, and he could hardly wait until tee-off time. When the day came, a huge crowd gathered to see the golfers play. The amateur was dressed to the nines, with his outfit coordinated even to his socks. His bag was the best, and he had the best clubs money could buy. When it was his turn, he stepped up to the first tee, took a mighty swing at his ball—a beautiful cut, if you please— and almost whiffed it. He got just enough of it to make it dribble off the tee. The old caddy who had to carry his huge bag for eighteen holes nudged his friend and said, "All bag. All bag." The amateur's outfit and equipment were making lots of clucking sounds, but when he tried to put the clubhead on the ball, it was obvious to everyone that there wasn't any nest.

The test is in the doing. Jesus said, "Not everyone who says to Me, 'Lord, Lord,' will enter the kingdom of heaven, but only he who does the will of My Father who is in heaven" (Matt. 7:21).

CHAPTER

Two

If Everybody's Doin' It, It Ain't Worth Much!

W hat enabled the church to triumph over the Roman Empire was not only the message of the Gospel; it was also that unyielding morality that would not accommodate the culture. Alexander Maclaren put it in these terms: "What was almost as powerful as the gospel of peace and love which the world proclaimed was a standard of austere morality which it held up to a world rotting in its own filth."

What is the weight that causes us to tilt toward doing things we know are beneath us or clearly wrong? What is the common appeal in our society? What is the justification of mediocrity? What is the enemy of excellence?

How about that old cliché, "Everybody's doin' it?" When our children come at us with this, we say, "I don't care if everyone is doing it—you're not going to!" But then we in our grown-up ways proceed to live like everyone else in our social circle. We want to fit into our neighborhood, our work scene, our larger society.

Yet, when we look at what everybody is supposedly doing, when we look at some events in history that were done by or at least agreed to by the majority, we see some less than wonderful things.

It was a majority who rejected the prophets, crucified Christ, burned Christians at the stake.

It was a majority who instituted slavery and even declared it a "divine institution."

It is easy for us to blame our leaders—the ones we choose—for what goes wrong. And sometimes they are blameable. We need for them to be persons of state. In Benjamin Franklin's day, a new politician was continually talking about his constituency, saying what they would or wouldn't like. And he wasn't talking about the high-minded people in his electorate.

Finally, Franklin had heard enough and told the man that he wasn't made a leader to try to find the lowest common denominator. "You are here to appeal to the finest and highest," he said. "If they don't like the way you do that, they'll take care of it."

It was the German poet Goethe who said that baseness appeals to the crowd. If you find something that everybody is doing quickly and easily, then you'll find something base.

But I think my grandmother put it better than any of them. When I went to her asking to do something because everyone else was doing it, she replied, "Well, if everybody's doin' it, it ain't worth much!"

Well, everybody's not doing it. Not in this generation or in any generation since God called Abraham and Sarah to be His people. From the time our God created a covenant people and called them by His name, there has been a righteous remnant of individuals who have kept the faith and have refused to lower their standards or accommodate their culture.

In the Book of Hebrews we read that Abraham said yes to God when he was told to leave his home and go to a strange land, even though he didn't know where he was going or why. Why did he do this? "He was looking forward to the city with foundations, whose architect and builder is God" (11:10). Abraham had seen a reason to hold steady, to follow the God who called him.

Dancing around the Golden Calf

I think about Moses who for forty years led the Children of Israel, and I wonder how he ever survived all the difficulties he had with them. You remember the story of Moses, up on the mountain with God, receiving the Ten Commandments. Meanwhile, down in the valley, the people decided they just couldn't wait any longer for Moses to return with word from this unseen God. They wanted a deity they could see and touch, and they persuaded Aaron to cast a god out of gold. When the golden calf was finished, the people danced around it and worshiped it.

This terrible scene reached up to God, who said to Moses, "Go back down, for the people have become corrupt." As Moses and Joshua made their way down and saw what was happening, Moses threw the two tablets against the mountain, breaking them to pieces. Then he ground the golden calf into powder and mixed it with water and made the people drink it.

Next he went to Aaron, his brother and the high priest, and demanded to know why he had let the people get out of control, and had made them a laughing-stock to their enemies. Aaron blamed it on the people, as if they *all* wanted the golden calf.

Moses knew this wasn't true, so he stood before the

27

people and called out, "Whoever is for the Lord, come to me" (Ex. 32:26). Many people quickly stepped forward to Moses. They wanted to follow the Lord and they would never dance around a golden calf.

Hundreds of years after Moses, King Nebuchadnezzar of Babylon besieged Jerusalem and carried back some of the finest young men to be trained to serve in his government. Four of these men still inspire us today—Daniel, Shadrach, Meshach, and Abednego. They were the ones who asked that they not be made to eat the king's rich food, because it was against their dietary laws. After Daniel interpreted some dreams for the king, he was made a ruler over a province of Babylon and the other three were made administrators in Babylon.

Not long after this, Nebuchadnezzar decided to make an image of gold, and he demanded that everyone bow down to it. Daniel must not have been in the area at the time, but his three friends were, and they refused to bow to the image when the trumpet signaled the correct time. The punishment for refusing was to be thrown into a fiery furnace. When the king heard that the three would not bow down, he was furious and he called them before him and asked, "Is this true? If you don't bow down, you will be thrown into the furnace, and what god can rescue you then?"

Shadrach, Meshach, and Abednego replied, "O Nebuchadnezzar, we do not need to defend ourselves before you in this matter. If we are thrown into the blazing furnace, the God we serve is able to save us from it, and He will rescue us from your hand, O king. But even if He does not, we want you to know, O king, that we will not serve your gods or worship the image of gold you have set up" (Dan. 3:16-18).

The Salt of the Earth
In every generation there are people like that. I recall a young man, Dennis Oetting, who moved to Houston while

working for the Westinghouse Corporation. At twenty-seven he was their leading salesman in Texas and was really on his way up. He wasn't here long before he got the "big call"—they were kicking him upstairs—moving him into a great position. He was definitely the fair-haired boy.

Dennis came to see me about this, because he was wrestling with another call—a really Big One, to preach the Gospel. He finally said yes to this one and no to the promotion, and then went back to school for four years. He is now a Methodist preacher who rejected wealth to follow God's higher and finer call.

I also think about a layman who has inspired and blessed me all his life—George Mayo. He was the district representative of his company, and also had a ministry in our church and conference, a ministry that we didn't think we could do without. One day the call came that George could become regional representative for his company and get a big boost in pay. He asked us to pray for him—his ministry was important to him, and if he took the job he would have to give it up.

After two weeks of praying and talking about it, George and his family decided that if they would be careful and maintain a modest lifestyle, they could live on the money he was already making, to enable him to turn down the promotion and keep his ministry.

I think too of a young man I buried from our church. He was gifted and personable and had been part of the advance group in George Bush's election campaign of 1988. Jay had graduated from the University of Texas, and then, with many options open to him, decided to invest his life shaping and forming young people as a schoolteacher.

The world will tell you, "Money makes the world go round. Everybody does their own thing." But the people I just mentioned did not; their first consideration is, "What is the will of God for my life?"

Do you sometimes feel as if you are the only one trying to hold up the light in a crooked and perverse generation? Do you succumb to self-pity saying, "I'm so lonely by myself in this office or in this crowd. I'm the only faithful one"?

When you go against the majority, you can end up feeling like Elijah did after he defeated the prophets of Baal. He thought he was the only champion Jehovah had in Israel. But God said, "Not so, Elijah. I have 7,000 people who haven't bowed the knee to Baal." God always has His people whose standards come from God, people who search His Scriptures, people who know about faithfulness and who prize virtue. These high-minded people choose to take the high road.

God has people we call "the salt of the earth." And that is what He wants all of us to be. In ancient days, salt was used as a preservative. And even today some of us enjoy country ham which has been salted and wrapped until it is cured.

When Jesus said, "You are the salt of the earth," He was saying that we, the righteous remnant of God, the followers of Jesus Christ, are what stands between our world and total decline.

When the people of the Roman Empire saw the way the early Christians lived, the way they did business and cared about each other and showed love and conducted their family life, many of them decided, "That's the only fit way to live."

We can't be constantly complaining about the sin here and the sinners there. The only thing the world really listens to and finds convincing is holiness. For holiness of life shows up the ugliness of sin.

A professor once told me a story about the ermine, that small animal whose pure white fur is prized for collars and for trim on judges' robes. He said that hunters would find the ermine's den and smear it with garbage and filth and then would turn the dogs loose. The dogs would chase the ermine right to his den. When he saw all that filth, the ermine stopped cold; he would face the fangs of the dogs rather than go in and soil his coat.

As Christians, we are called to be people who refuse to stain our souls. Paul charged Timothy to live a pure life. James said to keep ourselves unspotted from the world. And when Paul wrote, "Become blameless and pure, children of God without fault in a crooked and depraved generation, in which you shine like stars in the universe," he was talking to us (Phil. 2:15). He wanted us to be worth our salt!

When Salt Turns Bad

Before there was a king in Israel, the people of God had judges who ruled and defended them. The most famous of those judges was Samson, a man who had a special call from God. Before he was born, his parents were told that he would be a Nazirite. This meant that he would never drink anything intoxicating, would never have his hair cut, and would shun dead bodies. But more basic, he was to be separated to the Lord. Samson's mother took these vows for him, and also for herself while she was carrying him.

We don't know what Samson was thinking as he charged through his unruly life. Although he did free Israel from the domination of the Philistines, and in some measure fulfilled the purposes of God, he certainly did not live up to his vows. He was always sensual, giving in to his appetites.

What we know best about him is his relationship with Delilah, the third woman he was connected with. We are told that he truly loved her, but she clearly did not love him, and used him for the advantage of the Philistines. To do this, she had to discover the secret to his great strength. The first several times she asked, he told her lies. When he was asleep, someone would do what he had said, and then Delilah would call, "Samson, the Philistines are upon you!" Each time he would rise up and break the bonds they had put on him. And on each occasion he was apparently more dulled to the real motives of this conniving woman.

Samson finally told her the secret, for he was worn out from her nagging him about it. He said that if someone were to cut his hair, he would be powerless. You know what happened: she cut the hair and Samson got up as if to leave as he had done before, thinking nothing had changed. And it is here that we read the saddest verse in the Old Testament, "He did not know that the Lord had left him" (Jud. 16:20).

Samson had treated his vows and his calling from the Lord very lightly. He accomplished some of what God wanted done, but he lived an unholy life, and thought he could get by with this. If everybody was doing it, Samson would go them one better. He was so strong and inventive and persuasive that he could get what he wanted, to the sorrow of his parents. His life ended in tragedy, because he would not be faithful to God's calling.

Jesus talked about salt that could lose its saltiness. That is what happened to Samson. He started out well but lost his responsiveness to God somewhere along the line. Jesus said, 'If the salt loses its saltiness . . . it is no longer good for anything, except to be thrown out and trampled by men" (Matt. 5:13).

Either we are salting the world, for Christ's sake, or we are letting the world spoil us and rot us. The choice is ours.

A Vision of Greatness
It was historian Alfred North Whitehead who said that the foundation of our morality is a vision of greatness, and that

we need a habitual vision of greatness, for "the sense of greatness is the groundwork of morals."

There is a legend about an Indian chief who had to decide which of his four sons would succeed him. He gave them a contest. He said, "Each of you will run up the side of that mountain, and when you can't run anymore, pick a piece of vegetation to bring back, so that I will know how far up you went."

The first boy didn't go very far and brought back a twig of spruce. The second went a bit farther and brought back some mountain pine. The third boy went to the moss line and picked some chaparral.

The fourth son returned empty-handed, but with eyes shining. His feet were frostbitten and bleeding, but he didn't seem to notice, as he said to his father, "I went to the top of the mountain and saw the sea beyond it."

The chief said, "You will lead my people, for you have seen past the mountain and have a vision for what lies beyond."

As disciples of Christ, we are called to a vision of the city whose builder and maker is God—the Holy God who calls us to be holy. "Everybody's doing it" must not be part of our vocabulary anymore. We are children of the King!

CHAPTER

Three

Who Says Life Is
Supposed to Be Easy?

The first lesson we ought to teach our children is a lesson in reality. Life is never easy. Particularly in this decade of the 1990s, it is not easy for millions of people. The party of the 1980s is over, and we are struggling with the consequences and hoping for leaders who will be able to make some sense of our political and economic world.

And yet we all would like life to be easy. Most of us would be good members of the "now generation" as the young were called. We like instant everything. Instant and easy.

I heard of a minister who retired at age fifty-five, although he was in good health. I was surprised at this, since when you reach fifty you should be coming into your best years. His reason for retiring so early? "There are no easy churches anymore."

I knew another man who boasted as a teenager that by age fifty he would have all the money he needed and would be retired. Well, he made it. He retired before fifty, but all by himself. He had lost his family. His life is now a steady misery—the engine that was his life was revved up so high that now he can't shut it off. He doesn't know what to do with himself. He was just trying to have it easy.

It is tragic when we convey this sense of entitlement to our children and grandchildren, and teach them that they deserve to have it easy, and should be spared any struggle. Oh, we don't necessarily say this in words, but we say it in other ways, like explaining away their poor grades in elementary school, when they are just being lazy or refusing to concentrate. We say that the teacher doesn't like them or has it in for them, or that they are disrupted by other kids who are a bad influence on them.

When they are older, explaining it away becomes more difficult as, for instance, when they have been driving under the influence of alcohol. Yet Mom and Dad say, "Well, the policeman is picking on him. He just had a few beers. What's wrong with that?" So they rush down to the jail and hug their son and bail him out.

After that, it can get more serious yet. I recall a man who was finally arrested on a drug charge after the police tracked him. By then he was beyond the reach of his excusing family. All the things they did for him—all the shielding from responsibility, all their attempts to spare him the consequences of his behavior—all was done in "love."

When I was small, I had a favorite chicken we called Ole Blue. I was there when her chicks were hatching, and I saw that one was struggling to get out. Only his beak was protruding from the shell, and I could tell from the way it moved that he was working with all the energy he had. So I took my stubby finger and began to flick away parts of the broken shell. Finally, the little fellow was free, but he was a cripple the rest of his short life.

Just as the butterfly must struggle to emerge from the cocoon, so too our children need to learn that there is no easy way through life. If we protect them from the lessons of life, we produce cripples who are unable to stand up to the difficulties of the world. Even Mother Goose conveyed this reality, as in the line, "If wishes were horses, then beggars would ride."

There was a mind-set among our forebears in this country that reinforced reality. When Thomas Jefferson built the rotunda at the University of Virginia, he included a chemistry lab. Outside of the lab someone had to pump the bellows that kept the fire going, so that they could conduct experiments inside. The person chosen to work outside in the cold and rain or in the heat varied from month to month. The most undisciplined student in the class had to go out and pump the bellows. This made an indelible connection between the virtue of discipline and performance in school, and later performance in life.

Many people today have a television mentality. If they don't like what is on one channel, they touch the remote control and select another. Since much of what we see is unreal anyway, it is easy for children to begin to see the world apart from television in the same way; and think that if they don't like what is going on, they can just change channels — and without even stretching a muscle. The trouble with this is that when they go out to face the hard world, they find the remote control doesn't work. Then, they may take refuge in addictions, and we have all kinds today. When you ask someone who is addicted why they continue, they will tell you that they like the way it makes them feel. Someone along the line told them they were supposed to feel good all the time—someone, perhaps, who should have been taking responsibility for that person when he or she was young, and instead, taught the lie. Now the addict has a skewed perception of reality.

Our Example in Reality

When we look at the life of Jesus Christ, we see One who not only showed us what God the Father is like, but who also demonstrated for us what it is to be fully human and to embrace the struggle and survive. Jesus went through many situations in which He was deeply troubled. He was repeatedly tempted, He was denied, He was taunted, He was the object of public humiliation, and yet He remained strong and determined to fulfill His Father's will. He understood that God was at work in the difficult times, and He prayed, "Father, use Me to get glory for Yourself."

What a contrast between this attitude and the one we find today, even among many born-again Christians. There is a notion that the conversion experience is supposed to do all that is needed, and that life is easy coasting from then on. But that's not the way the Bible describes the Christian life, even if some preachers do.

When the Apostle Paul was writing to the Colossian Christians, he told them that Christ desired to present them to God "holy . . . , without blemish and free from accusation—if you continue in your faith, established and firm, not moved from the hope held out in the Gospel" (1:22-23). He wrote this because in the church of Colosse some of the members had strayed. Paul was telling them that just because they once stood before an altar of the church and took their vows of Christian discipleship, this didn't give a guarantee for the future. He said, "There is a proviso here."

We Methodists do not subscribe to the "once saved, always saved" doctrine, and we have taken quite a bit of static about this across the years. We just have never been able to accept that idea, because we fail to see that there is anything in the experience of grace that takes away our freedom. As long as we are free individuals, there is always the possibility of our falling. If we are not free to be damned, we are not free to be saved. You see, we take this matter of human freedom very seriously. Paul said, "Provided you continue stable and steadfast, not shifting from the hope of the Gospel."

Salvation means being rightly related to God through our Lord Jesus Christ in the experience of faith. In that relationship there is no magic that can repair in death what has been deliberately broken in life. Therefore, we must continue to work at the relationship with God. The writer of Hebrews asked, "How shall we escape if we ignore such a great salvation?" (2:3) We receive this salvation as a marvelous gift, not to put it on a shelf and adore it, but to work at it. Another way of putting it is to say, "We are saved, and we have the witness of the Holy Spirit with our spirit that our sins have been forgiven. Not only are we saved, but we are also *being* saved."

Christian maturity involves a lifelong process. When we forget this, something deadly happens. There just aren't any shortcuts to the real Christian life.

Connecting Time and Eternity
Do you see the connection between the way we think about this life and the way we approach eternal life? I heard a while ago that a friend of mine had walked out on his wife and family. When I asked him why in the world he had done this, he replied, "We were having a hard time and I wasn't happy."

My first concern for any marriage, for your marriage, is not happiness. My first concern is for the state of your commitment. If your commitment is intact, your happiness

41

will take care of itself in most cases.

Every time I go to a fiftieth wedding anniversary party, and I observe the gray hairs and lines and creases on the faces of the couple, I think that each line is a badge of honor to some struggle, some battle in that relationship. That's the way real life is. We need to stop running from the struggle and begin to embrace it. We need to see glory in it.

If we are unhappy all the time, we need to make some changes, to realign, perhaps to renegotiate a relationship. But we are still going to have to embrace the struggle if we are ever going to see God's glory in it. And yes, God is in the struggle. Jesus prayed, "I can't ask that You take Me out of the struggle. For this reason, I came to this hour." You can read His prayer just before His death in John 17. Jesus embraced the struggle and found God was glorified.

The Apostle Paul asked that God would remove the thorn in his flesh. Likely it was a physical ailment, perhaps a problem with his eyes. After Paul prayed three times, God answered him, "That's yours, Paul, to bear for Me. But it is not yours alone. My grace is going to be sufficient for you and My power will be made perfect in your weakness." Paul accepted this answer and said, "Therefore I will boast all the more gladly about my weaknesses, so that Christ's power may rest on me. That is why, for Christ's sake, I delight in weaknesses, in insults, in hardships, in persecutions, in difficulties. For when I am weak, then I am strong" (2 Cor. 12:9-10).

Asking the Right Questions

Opera singer Beverly Sills has known the realities of life. Her first child was born almost totally deaf. A few years later, her second child was born with Down's syndrome. It was then that Beverly took a year off to come to terms with life. During this time, she discovered that she was asking the wrong question, one that was tearing her apart as it came from her heart over and over, "Why me, Lord? Why me?" But then she came to a second question, "Why them? Why them?"

We do live in a fallen and imperfect world that is far different than our Creator intended. Sin has put things out of gear. Because of this, we all take our lumps just from being alive in this world. When Beverly came to terms with the real nature of life in a fallen world, then she was able to continue her life of artistry.

We all need to come to the place where we can see value in the struggle. In the Book of Hebrews we read that even though Christ was the Son of God, yet He learned obedience by the things that He suffered.

It was the Apostle Peter who wrote to the suffering Christians of his day, encouraging them to endure. "And the God of all grace, who called you to His eternal glory in Christ, after you have suffered a little while, will Himself restore you and make you strong, firm, and steadfast. To Him be the power for ever and ever. Amen" (1 Peter 5:10).

If enduring the struggle has this kind of result, how in the world can we believe that we can develop strong character without some hard times? Why do we buy into our society's Creed of Fast and Easy?

We are seeing more teenage suicides today than ever before. I believe one of the reasons for this is that teens are afraid of living. Life is the scariest proposition of all for people who have bought into the lie that it is supposed to be easy, and then they find out it is hard.

It was Karl Jung, the great Swiss psychiatrist, who said that there are some problems you just have. It is not in our power or the power of the world to solve them. And the greatest problems cannot be solved; rather, they must be outgrown. And to do this is to rise above them.

How Do We Continue the Struggle?

How do we continue being stable and steadfast? How do we find the motivation to keep on struggling to present ourselves faithful to Christ? How do we conform to His image? We know we fall so far short of all this. The Apostle Paul found his motivation in knowing that somehow he was an extension of Christ in this world. He said that in his body he completed "what is still lacking in regard to Christ's afflictions, for the sake of His body, which is the church" (Col. 1:24). He knew that his mission was to complete that which Christ was doing in His body while He was on earth.

I have never seen people leave off the struggle when they really understood that they are called to be an extension of Jesus in the world.

Do you remember the story of husband-wife team Pierre and Marie Curie, the French scientists who discovered radium? They worked closely together in their laboratory until the day when absent-minded Pierre walked in front of a wagon and was run over and killed. Marie was devastated. He had only recently been appointed to a prestigious chair in the Academy of Science.

A few days after Pierre's death, Marie was invited to take the chair, and she accepted with gratitude. A great scientist in her own right, she entered the hall that day to an overflow crowd. They all wondered, "What will she say? Will she eulogize her husband?" She began reading, " . . . when I consider the vast progress which science has made. . . . " The crowd was startled. Then they realized that she picked up exactly where Pierre had left off when he had been interrupted while reading a paper he was presenting to them.

As Christians, we should bear with pride the fact that we pick up where Jesus left off, because we are His body in the world. Years ago, a certain moving company moved the treasures of King Tut when they were shown in museums in America. The sides of the vans boasted, "We moved a king's treasure." This is the joy of the Christian. We move a King's treasure in these earthen vessels of our bodies. When we stumble and fall and fail Him again and again, still He can use us to advance the cause of Christ in the world.

In his historical novel, *The Agony and the Ecstasy,* Irving Stone told how Pope Julius had given Michelangelo a most difficult assignment. The sculptor was to go to the blue hills of Carrara and quarry out a tomb for the pope. Michelangelo selected Gilberto, the finest foreman available in all of Italy. They hired a fine crew and set out to fulfill the task. For a long time they labored, but finally the crew gave up. Gilberto spoke for them all when he said to Michelangelo, "We've had it. We've tried. It's enough. We can't do it. We're quitting."

Michelangelo looked him steadily in the eye and said, "I can understand if you must quit, but I hope you will understand when I say that I cannot quit. I will find another crew. I will find another foreman. And then I will come back and complete the task, because I am under the assignment of the Holy Father."

That was how Paul continued on—he knew himself to be under the commission of Christ. This kind of mature faith is not the result of a single experience, but of many campaigns and battles and victories. We reach such maturity when we deliberately and intentionally share our lives with Christ, when we learn to rest in His reliability and experience the sufficiency of His presence.

It was the Old Testament Prophet Micah who spoke of the miseries that Israel had experienced. But then he said,

But as for me, I keep watch for the Lord,
I wait in hope for God my Savior;
my God will hear me.

45

Do not gloat over me, my enemy!
Though I have fallen, I will rise.
Though I sit in darkness,
the Lord will be my light (7:7-8).

Sure, there will be struggle. Sure, you will fall at times. Sure, you're going to sit in darkness, just as Micah did. But you too can watch in hope for the Lord and know that He will give you light for your darkness and strength for your struggles.

CHAPTER

Four

Making Time for
What Matters Most

We all have weeks when we are tired and want to quit. One time when I was having the blahs, I thought about my son and my son-in-law, who plan to practice medicine together and live out in the country with their families, a short way from the town where they would practice. They would have a lake and lots of dogs. There would be gardens and a fruit orchard. They would build houses on their lake and, according to their plans, would reserve a place for my wife and me.

Sometimes when I get tired, I move off to the lake in my mind. I start thinking about when I am going to walk away from all the work that is in front of me every day. When I was much younger, I couldn't think about that, but now I do; and it takes an exercise of will to put myself back into the present, and to continue my God-given responsibilities.

As I look around, I see lots of people who are afflicted with the blahs, and it seems to me that many of them are just hanging on, instead of going on. In the process they are losing fifteen or twenty years of their lives. It was James Carroll who said, "Our commitment to the transcendent is the refusal to allow the best years of our lives to happen without us."

One time when I boarded a plane for Dallas, the flight attendant started giving the landing speech instead of the take-off speech. Halfway through she caught herself and everybody began laughing. I wanted to console her, to say, "Don't feel bad about it. All my life I have known people who've talked about landing and yet have never taken off. I know people who are talking about retirement but who have never been active. I know people who are talking about the life hereafter, but who have never had life here."

What Is This Quantity Called Time?

Someone has calculated that we spend twenty-five years working, twenty-five years sleeping, seven years playing, six years eating, five years getting ready, three years waiting, and one year on the telephone. Of course, for some people, the telephone figure would be considerably higher!

When you add up the way you spend your lifetime, you may think, "I don't have much time for creativity, or for what I want to do." You may feel like the rabbit in *Alice in Wonderland* who always ran around looking at his watch and exclaiming, "I'm late, I'm late, I'm late for an important date!"

For many adults who are part of the Baby Boom generation, the single most valuable commodity is time. They are very careful of how they spend their free time and won't give away blocks of it to any person or group, unless they feel they are getting enough in return. This includes time spent at church. It has to be worth their while.

I read an article in the *New Yorker* magazine about Billy Bob's nightclub in Fort Worth. At Billy Bob's there is a machine called "What's your excuse?" When you put in a dollar, you can choose from fifteen different background sounds. Then, when you make a call, you can say, "I am still at the office" and hear office sounds in the background. Or, you can call and say, "I am at the stockyard" and hear mooing cattle. The one most often used is, "I am at church." On this one, you can get sounds of an organ and even the murmur of the congregation.

Now you can buy a version of this machine to attach to your own phone at home—canned sounds for giving an illusion about how you are using your time.

We all operate with illusions about time—about how much we have, and how we are using it. I heard about some college students who were getting ready for Parents' Weekend. A popular student hangout that sold beer and pizza was also getting ready. It put a sign in the window that said, "Bring your parents here and we'll pretend we don't know you." Then the pastor of the village church got into the act; he put out a sign that read, "Bring your parents here and we'll pretend we know you."

Some people are under the illusion that time will take care of hurts, will heal, will give them maturity or wisdom. My wife and I went to a high school reunion a few years ago and saw a woman who had made the cheerleading squad in the 1950s. We sat near her for about two hours at the reunion and discovered that she still thinks of herself as a cheerleader. Now that was fine in the 1950s, but for someone past fifty, it's not very becoming.

Preparing for a Time of Harvest
There is nothing in the passing of time that will produce wholeness. If we want it, we need to be sowing the seeds

of wholeness. Time is like the ground where we plant the seeds for the harvest we hope to reap in the future. When the Apostle Paul wrote to the Galatian Christians, he gave them a principle that applies to time and also to the illusions we often have about it. He said, "Do not be deceived: God cannot be mocked. A man reaps what he sows" (6:7).

It was Thoreau who said, "We act as though we could kill time without injuring eternity." We choose how we use our time, whether we think so or not. Time should be our servant, not our master. As Christians we cannot afford to pretend about what time is and does. Time is not necessarily our friend. Time simply presents the harvest which we have sown, whether it is good or bad.

This is why it is so important to be honest and sincere as we think about time and the ways we spend it. I often think about the statement that Abraham Lincoln was said to have made in 1858, "You can fool all the people some of the time, and some of the people all the time, but you cannot fool all the people all of the time." However, the fourth part of the statement is generally left off: "And you can't fool God any of the time." God knows what kind of a harvest time is going to bring you, whether it will be good or bad, and whether or not you are doing anything to make it a good harvest.

My brother and I used to share responsibility for milking the cows when we were boys. After we finished milking, we had to get them into the right pasture. You see, there was a field full of weeds with a small yellow flower that was very bitter to the taste. For some reason I can't figure out, the cows loved to eat that flower. Nobody had to tell our parents if we got careless about where we put the cows. All they had to do was to spread the butter on the toast or drink some of the milk, and they knew where the cows had been grazing.

There will come a day when it will be manifestly plain,

to God and to the whole world, what pasture we have been grazing in. Time is going to bring that harvest. Therefore, we need to be honest with God and with ourselves. Paul emphasizes in his letter to the Galatians:

The one who sows to please his sinful nature, from that nature will reap destruction; the one who sows to please the Spirit, from the Spirit will reap eternal life. Let us not become weary in doing good, for at the proper time we will reap a harvest if we do not give up. Therefore, as we have opportunity, let us do good to all people, especially to those who belong to the family of believers (6:8-10).

Chronos Time and Kairos Time

In the Bible we read about two kinds of time that are occurring simultaneously. Chronos time is chronological time, what we mark off on our calendars. This kind of time progresses in a straight line, but it is also circular, in that we move in orderly months and years that are marked off by the sun and moon and the seasons. We might think of it as large spirals moving down a line.

Kairos time has to do with fulfillment and fullness. There is a time that is never repeated. Kairos has to do with appointed times, and is spoken of in relation to prophecies and their fulfillment. We read that when the fullness of time came, Jesus came to earth. It was kairos time that Jesus was talking about when He said that His hour had not come, and then later that it had come, as He approached the cross.

The kairos moments and days happen within the chronos time, and sometimes we don't recognize them. In fact, far too often we don't. They come to us in the routines of life when we are busy with other things and are not expecting the extraordinary. Such moments come

53

more often to those who know that they may happen at any moment.

If you are a parent or if you work with children, you know that the most wonderful encounters happen suddenly, as if by accident, when you are least expecting them. And they remind you to be open to such experiences more often, because the children grow up so quickly and are gone.

In our church, we have confirmation classes once a year for those children who are ready to join the church. At the close of one such class recently, we had a special Saturday morning to which we invited all the children and their parents. During that morning, we played games, read the Bible, talked about prayer, and made pretzels into one of the symbols of prayer. Then we went to the chapel and all celebrated Communion.

As I watched those parents, I felt proud, because I knew they all had so many things to do at home or with their other children on a Saturday. But they were in a kairos moment. They were seizing the appointed time that never could be repeated. They wanted the Christian faith implanted in their children and on this Saturday morning they were giving their support to this desire. They were letting their children know how important it is to be a Christian and to make personal confession of that faith.

I think with sadness of other parents who have ignored the time of God's appointing with their children, at home and at church. They have said, "Oh, he'll grow out of it." or "She is just in a phase." Of course, they'll grow out of it. They will become adults, but with the same attitudes and behaviors that have gone on in the past, only worse. It is crucial that parents and grandparents and teachers meet the moment with the children in their lives, that kairos time which cannot be repeated, cannot be recalled. There is nothing more important.

We live in a society where there is profound biblical illiteracy. I read a story about a man who went to a jewelry store to buy a cross. He told the young clerk he would like to buy a gold cross. The clerk hesitated a moment and then asked, "Do you want a plain one or one with a little man on it?"

If we do not teach this generation who the "little man" is, if they do not learn the good news that this man Jesus lived and died for our sins and rose again from the dead, we are sending them into the world unprepared for life. It is like putting a child into a pasteboard box and sending him adrift on the open sea. We must make time for what matters. Kairos time comes, passes, and is gone.

The Future Feast of the Harvest

There will come a time when the only show in town will be serving God day and night. But before this day comes, there will be a judgment in which all that is hidden will be brought to light. Before the judgment seat of Christ we will all give account to God for our lives. What we have sown over the years will be very obvious.

If as confessing believers we are not exempt from the final judgment, what is our distinction? It is that we come to the day of judgment clothed in the salvation Christ came to offer. We will come as those who have accepted the forgiveness of Jesus Christ, not as those who have rejected it. We will come not in lonely isolation, but in the company of our Advocate, Jesus Christ the Righteous, who will personally plead our case.

We are to live now in light of that last day when we stand before God. He is the Master of time and He has given us enough time to do His will. On that last chronos day, the trumpet of the Lord will sound and time will be no more. Chronos time isn't going to make it into heaven. No wristwatches there, no alarm clocks. And as we live today, we should make time our servant, not our master. Chronos time has a limited lifespan. We are going to survive it, even if it doesn't always feel that way.

In the Old Testament, the Hebrew people celebrated a harvest festival called the Feast of Tabernacles. As part of the celebration, the people waved palm branches in thanksgiving that the seeds they planted had grown and yielded a good harvest. They had now reaped what they had sown.

The Feast of Tabernacles was also for remembering the past. The people remembered that God had led them through the sea, through the desert, through the wilderness, through so many difficult experiences, and had brought them at last to the Promised Land. Whatever they endured, whatever price they paid, was as nothing compared to the joy of being God's people. Have you reached the point where you can bless God for all the tough experiences that drew you closer to Him?

In the Book of Revelation there is a scene in which a great number of people are standing before the throne of God and in front of the Lamb of God, Jesus Christ. They are all wearing white robes, and they are holding palm branches in their hands. These people come from all countries, all tribes, all languages, and together they're celebrating the final harvest. They cry out together, "Salvation belongs to our God, who sits on the throne, and to the Lamb." And then the angels and the creatures of heaven join in to worship, "Amen! Praise and glory and wisdom and thanks and honor and power and strength be to our God forever and ever. Amen!" (Rev. 7:10-12)

Jesus Himself was put into the ground as a seed, and He came up from the ground of death as a plant whose branches would heal every person who comes to Him.

Will you be in that final harvest celebration?

CHAPTER

Five

Who Really Cares about Me?

We all have days when we feel that no one cares about us, that it doesn't really matter to anyone whether we live or die. For most of us such a feeling is little more than a passing mood. But many people have reason to ask whether anyone really does care. And after they ask long enough, they can begin to despair of life itself.

You have seen the "Dear Abby" columns in the newspaper, in which she answers the many problems sent to her. From time to time, she will conclude a piece of advice with two words, "I care." It doesn't matter that it is impersonal and on the back page of the newspaper. It doesn't matter that the column is read by millions. The world is so hungry to know that somebody cares that they love to see those words, no matter where they are.

You may remember the movie actor William Holden. When I read about his death some years ago, I felt sad about the circumstances surrounding it. Mr. Holden had been very successful and lived his later years in luxury. He had a palace in Palm Springs, another home in Los Angeles, and his own hunting preserve in Africa.

At the time of his death, he was in California and was missed by his doorman who recalled seeing Mr. Holden go into the building some days before. When the doorman entered the apartment, he found that Holden had fallen and hit his head, and had probably been dead for several days. He had everything in terms of material goods and popularity, but he didn't have anyone who kept him in mind enough to miss him until days had passed.

What happened to him is a fear that plagues older people especially—not just getting sick or being hurt, but that there will be no one close to care for them.

In one of my earlier churches, we organized a caregiving program. One of our caregivers went to see a senior citizen who was homebound and discovered that the woman had been paralyzed by a stroke and was lying in her bed completely conscious but unable to reach the telephone, unable to even cover herself to keep warm, unable to get water or food. All she could do was to lie there and wait. The caregiver saw that she got the medical help she needed. But we all asked ourselves, "What if our church hadn't been there to care?"

Feeling Connected to the Church

Lots of people go to church quite regularly, but they don't feel very connected to it. They don't have people there who really know them or care about their concerns. In a large church that feeling can be accentuated, because they have to work harder to get acquainted.

In Methodism, we have a unique tradition begun by John Wesley, who divided his converts into small groups for their Christian growth and encouragement. One of these groups was called a *band* in which three to five people met regularly to encourage one another in the faith. A second type of group was called a *class*, in which eight to fifteen persons met to hold one another accountable in spiritual growth and ministry. A third type was called the *society*, which was a larger gathering for worship, celebration, and encouragement.

Wesley's groups always included encouragement, for this is a sacred agenda for the Christian. The Apostle Paul wrote to the church at Thessalonica, "Therefore encourage one another and build each other up, just as in fact you are doing" (1 Thes. 5:11). In the New Testament, there are many other verses that speak of the importance of encouraging one another, and there is no time that we need this more than when we feel no one cares.

However, it is difficult to receive that kind of encouragement if you are not connected to the church in a vital way, if you have not joined yourself to a group of people who come together for the purpose of caring about one another—and not just when there are critical needs.

In our church in Houston, we have sixty-four Home Groups that meet together each week. In each group eight to twelve people study the Bible, have fun together, share their concerns, pray for each other, sometimes eat a little, and usually love each other a lot. When they join a Home Group, members covenant together to the following:

- to commit to the group, with attendance a priority
- to give support and encouragement to the group
- to share stories of their faith journeys
- to hold in confidence all that is shared
- to give others permission to ask for help and prayer

- to grow in faith, love, and the mission of Jesus Christ
- to bring friends and neighbors into the fellowship

Rosalie is a member of a home group. When her beloved nephew died, her group came together the night before the burial to support and sustain her. Rosalie said, "God's love flowed unendingly through each of these as they surrounded me in my need." But if Rosalie hadn't connected herself to the church in this intimate and vital way, the encouragement wouldn't have been there for her.

Don't wait until you have a dire need to think about connection. Your church may already have small groups. And if it doesn't, perhaps you can be part of making them happen.

I love the story about the boy who went to Sunday School and heard for the first time about the Good Samaritan. When he came home, his mother asked what he had learned. He told her about the man who was traveling to Jericho and fell among thieves who left him wounded and bleeding and lying in the ditch. He told her of the priest and the Levite who walked on the other side, and finally, of the Samaritan who stopped and bandaged his wounds and put him on his own donkey and took him to an inn and left money to care for him.

After the boy had recited the story, his mother asked, "And what did you learn from this?" To which he replied, "If I ever get into trouble, I can expect somebody to come and help me." I think it is all right to turn the application that way. People in the family of God should have such an expectation. But in our modern world, with distances and mobility as they are, and with the fast pace of life, we need to do our part and be sure we are connected to the life of the church, not only in worship and service, but also in that spiritual work of encouragement. For most people, this work takes place in a small group. The larger church just can't handle it—in many cases it doesn't even know when there is a need.

I will never forget the night when a rather new Christian who had just joined the church and also a Sunday School class rushed to the hospital with his wife. They were expecting their first child, and now the baby was about to be born prematurely. Word was quickly spread through the Sunday School class, and many of the members gathered in the hospital waiting room.

When the baby was born, she lived only a few minutes. After embracing his tearful wife, the young husband walked blindly through the doors into the waiting room. In his grief, he was determined to be alone. But when he had to walk through the members of his Sunday School class to get to the darkness of the night, he was changed forever. He told me later that the concern on the faces of his brothers and sisters in Christ, and the love he felt as they reached out to him, was a life-transforming experience.

Caring through Serving

I know of a layman who is making a terrific impact for good and for the Lord in his city. It was my joy to baptize this man some years ago, and I will never forget how he asked that a certain usher come and stand with him at his baptism. The layman told me later, "I would like to be able to say that it is because of you and your preaching that I joined this church, but that isn't so. The first time I entered this building, I didn't think I could stay—I was so lonely, so afraid. But this usher saw me and took me under his wing, asked me to sit beside him, later introduced me to his friends, and then took me to his Sunday School class. I am here because this man reached out and took my hand."

Sometimes we don't think that ushering is as important as other ministries in the church, but it can be. This usher saw his service not merely as getting people to the right pew and taking the offering, but as a way to connect and to care.

In 1992 I modified my ministry because of a study I did on the life of Moses. As Moses began to lead the Children of Israel, he tried to do too much himself. His father-in-law, Jethro, saw that he was wearing himself out trying to handle the smallest problems; and he helped Moses see that a leader who had been called by God could better serve his people by taking their concerns to God in prayer. Elders chosen from among the people could deal with details on a daily basis.

Early in 1992, I began to pray for each member of my church by name. I would write a letter telling the member that in ten days I would be praying for them, and I invited the member to send me specific concerns. In my letter, I assured the individual that I would be praying for him or her by name, to please contact me in order to guide me in my prayers.

The response to this has been overwhelming. My own prayer life has been enriched, and the discipline of prayer has become much more real to me through this intercession. Many of our people have said that they have been blessed by knowing that their pastor prayed for them by name, in a very specific time and place. After reading my letter, one man became so convicted about his indifference toward the church that he decided to give the church a beautiful ranch, which is now our Spiritual Life Retreat Center.

A woman called our congregation recently and told me, "I can't talk very loudly or he'll hear me. I'm on the upstairs phone and I just have to talk to someone." She went on to explain that her husband was suffering from Alzheimer's disease and had been for five years. The disease was taking its toll on him, on her, and on all the family. The children used to make frequent trips to see them, but his condition now caused unpredictable violence, and the children had stopped coming. She said, "This man treated me wonderfully for forty-five years. We traveled and raised our family together, and we were good friends. I know we still are—he looks like the man I lived with all those years—but yesterday he pulled a knife on me."

She said she had been unable to attend church for nearly two and one-half years and could rarely leave her home. Her husband required constant supervision, and she couldn't afford nursing care.

After I talked with her, we decided to start an Alzheimer's Support Group at the church, and invited those in the congregation with need to join us. Very slowly, people are beginning to claim their need for help. We are training persons who can go into a home and assist in these situations by tending the patient while the caregiver goes out for dinner or shopping.

God's Life-Support System

Have you ever thought about how God intended to care for all He created? When Jesus spoke to the people in what we call the Sermon on the Mount, He urged them not to be anxious about their physical needs. To make His point, He pointed to the flowers around them, and to the birds flying above them. He said that the birds didn't sow or reap or store crops in barns, but that God fed them. That the lilies of the field did not labor or spin, but that Solomon in all his splendor was not dressed like one of these.

And then Jesus told them that they were of so much more value than the beauties of nature, and that their Heavenly Father would care for them.

However, when it comes to human beings, God's support system usually works through other people. In the Old Testament we read how God wanted Israel to live together in tribes and clans and families and to show special care for those with needs. In His ministry, Jesus emphasized showing love and care for those who could not meet their own needs. In the early days of the church, there was a wonderfully open sharing of money and property and time so that all were cared for.

But all this caring depends on being connected to the people of God. I remember the story of the little boy who was asked to lead in prayer at family devotions one night when the extended family was present. The boy began to pray in loud and ringing tones describing vividly all the things he wanted for his birthday. When he finished, his father took him aside and gently reminded him that he didn't have to talk so loudly when he prayed, that God wasn't a long way off, and could hear even a whisper. The little boy said, "I know that, Dad, but Grandpa can't."

One of the ways we know that God can hear us is when His people hear us. Yes, there are times when we have the assurance only in our hearts, and God can make His presence and provision known in any manner He chooses. But He has designed that we be in fellowship with His people, not only for worship but also for encouragement and growth and mutual care.

It isn't enough for us to have our physical needs met. We also want to feel that we are cared for. We are like Boswell, the biographer of the famed Samuel Johnson. Boswell was very unsure how the great Johnson felt about him. He wondered if Johnson respected him and loved him, and so he began to plague him with questions to find out how he stood with him.

Finally, one day Johnson said to Boswell, "Take out your notebook. Write in it, *I am held in highest esteem.*" When Boswell finished writing, Johnson said to him, "That, Sir, is true. That is true until you're asked to erase what you have written."

God knows how often we need to hear this. He has said it to us by creating us in His image, by sending us His Son, by offering Jesus for our redemption from sin. But the way we most clearly understand the value God places on us is in the fellowship of other Christians who live out this estimate that God has of us. God loves us with an enduring love in Jesus Christ, and He has signed it in His own blood and given us the Cross as the ultimate sign of His continuing concern for us.

I was twenty years old when I went to be Miss Crawley's pastor. She lived in a trailer and washed eggs for her son who raised laying hens. One day she gave me a silver dollar and asked me to carry it in my pocket to remind me that someday she was going to die and then I was going to have to preach her funeral.

It was three years later, while I was in seminary, that I got the call that she had died, and I drove 300 miles to speak at her funeral. The next week I got a letter from her son. He could neither read nor write, and he had someone write the letter for him. In the last paragraph he said, "Just remember this, if you ever need me, just call me." Then there was an X, the signature of someone who cannot write his name.

I was touched by that because I know that I have a claim on that man's life because of my relationship to his mother.

God invites us to call on His Son when we need Him, and He signs the invitation not with an X but with the blood of the cross. Every day we keep in mind His sacrificial work on Calvary's cross to remind us that we are loved by One who cares about us and who wants His love to transform our living.

CHAPTER

Six

Ordinary People — A Tonic for What Ails Us

I grew up in the era of tonic tune-ups for the start of the school year. I believe my brothers and sisters and I took every tonic the Watkins man delivered to our house—and my mother tried them all. I never tasted one that wasn't ghastly.

Not long ago, I asked my mother about the one we used to take in August to tune us up for the school year, to make sure we wouldn't get sick. She thought its number was 666. That's the number of the beast, and certainly fits everything I remember about the tonic. It was so effective that it could take a young boy enjoying the last barefoot days of summer and make me anxious for school to start just so I could leave off the tonic. When we would get through September and October and even November without a cold, my mother would be reinforced in thinking it was the tonic—"It works every time!"

We all need a tonic now and then to help us feel in the pink, to bring us to our maximum efficiency as persons. The Apostle Paul knew about this, and never more than when he was in a Roman prison thinking about two former supporters who had deserted him in his time of need. They might have been ashamed of his chains, or felt that it was just too dangerous to be associated with a man in prison. There were others who left him too, but for some reason he mentioned these two by name—Phygellus and Hermogenes.

And then a young man named Onesiphorus appeared and visited him again and again, and those visits were like a breath of fresh air. Paul said his visits braced him up, they cheered him, and that Onesiphorus was not ashamed of his chains, but took great pains to be helpful to him.

Besides being in prison, Paul was at his wit's end about the church in Corinth, for the people there gave him more trouble than any other church. Some of the members were grossly immoral, and he had to confront them about the way they were living, and call them and the whole church to repentance for tolerating this sinful behavior.

Someone once said that two people you should avoid at all costs are a timid surgeon and a timid preacher, since neither one can do you any good. And Phillips Brooks said that if a preacher is afraid that what he is going to preach will make his people mad at him, and if that turns him away, he ought to go and sell shoes. There is no place for him in the pulpit.

Indeed, the Apostle Paul was not timid, but he was lonely. He was an authentic person, but he still felt like the rest of us in the ministry—we want to be liked. One of the reasons I struggled against going into the ministry was that I didn't think I could be a preacher and also be real. And then I found out in my own pastor and in the Apostle

Paul that reality and authenticity can go together.

Paul had another visitor while he was in prison, a young man named Onesimus, who proved to be very helpful to him. Paul called Onesimus a dearly loved brother. And the surprising thing about this young man is that he was a runaway slave, and we know of him because Paul wrote to his owner, Philemon, to say that he was sending Onesimus back to Colossae, but hoped that Philemon would return him to Rome to minister to him.

Another time when Paul had a bad case of the mullygrubs and needed a pickup, he was in Macedonia. We know he was feeling down because of what he wrote to the Corinthian church—yes, the very ones who had caused him such pains. "When we came into Macedonia, this body of ours had no rest, but we were harassed at every turn—conflicts on the outside, fears within. But God, who comforts the downcast, comforted us by the coming of Titus, and not only by his coming but also by the comfort you had given him. He told us about your longing for me, your deep sorrow, your ardent concern for me, so that my joy was greater than ever" (2 Cor. 7:5-8).

The Descendants of Barnabas

After Paul was converted, the Christians were not eager to receive him. To them, he was still Saul of Tarsus, the enemy of the church. And we can only wonder what would have become of him, except for Barnabas. Following his conversion, Saul tried to become part of the fellowship of the church, but no one wanted anything to do with him, and who can blame them? For Saul had been laying waste the church by persecuting its people.

In the Book of Acts we read that Barnabas "took him" and brought him into the fellowship so that Paul felt included. It is possible that we would never have heard of Saul of Tarsus, much less the Apostle Paul, had it not been

73

for Barnabas, Son of Encouragement.

In our church we have a Barnabas Society, people who become friends with our newest members, and for at least six months make a special effort to talk with them on a regular basis and help them integrate into the life of the church. New Christians have always been dependent on the descendants of Barnabas to help them find their place in the body of Christ.

When I entered the ministry, I didn't know anyone at the first denominational conference I attended. One pastor saw my confusion and aloneness and asked me if I had anywhere to stay. I said that I didn't yet, and he responded, "You do now," and took me to his motel room. The motel was already full, and my friend slept on the carpet those nights because so many delegates were staying in his room.

That was more than thirty years ago. My friend has since died, and I officiated at his funeral. Every person who stayed in that motel room has been a lifelong friend of mine. I felt so much more secure at that conference and also in my first appointment because I had a friend.

Ordinary People

None of the great friends of Paul preached sermons which were recorded in Holy Scripture. Their names are not household words, and none of them has a famous building named after him. However, as we study Scripture, and as we observe life, we understand that ordinary people are the real stars among us, ordinary people who are extraordinary in reaching out to help, to encourage, and to lift others. This is a universal gift that God has given to us all. We may not be famous saints, but we have been given the gift of friendship and encouragement that makes us saints in the shadows.

Paul was praying for God to do something great for him,

and in walked Titus, a common ordinary person. Have you ever thought how wonderful it is that our God uses ordinary people to breathe new life into other people? Many times we are waiting for some spectacular miracle, while that very miracle is knocking on our door in the person of a neighbor. A loving Christian friend comes to us in our hour of need.

Even Jesus had low times. Imagine how He must have been feeling when He said, "Now is My soul heavy." God comforted Him through that little group with whom He lived and ministered, that band of ordinary people who clearly didn't have life all together. They failed Jesus in many ways and misunderstood Him. And yet, when He came to the end of His life, He was grateful to them and said, "You are those who have continued with Me in My trials. You have been with Me in the ups and downs of My life." Nothing can take the place of that. God uses ordinary people to bring new life and heart into other people.

Just think how God used Esau to bring new heart into his twin brother, Jacob. Because Esau was the older of the two, he should have gotten the lion's share of the inheritance and his father's best blessings. But Jacob tricked his father and got the blessings of the birthright. Esau was so angry that Jacob had to flee for his life and went to the home of a relative, where he worked and eventually married two sisters. He continued in his slippery ways, even tricking his father-in-law, Laban, who was himself a pretty slippery character. By the time Jacob and his then large family left Laban's home, they were wealthy people.

And now, Jacob was going to have to face Esau whom he had cheated twenty years earlier. He was terrified and thought that if he sent some of his herds on ahead and offered them to Esau, maybe he would appease his wrath.

On the night before the dreaded encounter, Jacob had an encounter with God by the Jabbok brook that transformed his life and gave him a new name, Israel. He was a new man, but he still had to contend with his brother. That's how it is with us too. We have to deal with some of those old sins and conflicts even after we have new life.

When the two brothers met, Esau asked why Jacob had sent all the presents, and Jacob responded that he wanted to find favor in Esau's eyes. Then Esau said, "I already have plenty, my brother. Keep what you have for yourself." To which Jacob responded, "No, please! If I have found favor in your eyes, accept this gift from me. For to see your face is like seeing the face of God, now that you have received me favorably" (Gen. 33:9-10). Why did Jacob say that seeing Esau was like seeing the face of God? Because in spite of all the wrong that Jacob had done, Esau still called him "brother." He forgave him and loved him.

God had done all that He could do for Jacob when they wrestled all night and then God blessed him. There was something else Jacob needed, and the only person who could give it to him was his brother. That moment of meeting was like a tonic to Jacob's soul. Things were right again between him and his brother.

Close Encounters
In 1967 when I returned to graduate school in preparation for writing my dissertation, I met a man who was also about ten years older than most of the students. I was commuting from my church and found that my time at the university was quite lonely. But what I didn't realize was that it was far more lonely for my new friend, Fred, because he was the only black man in the class.

One day I saw him walking along slowly after class and asked him if he would like to have lunch with me. Over lunch we talked about our parish experiences and so enjoyed our time together that we did it again and again, and soon became close friends.

It was during one of those lunches that Fred asked if I would preach for him in his church, something I was happy to do. As he introduced me that morning, I was nearly wiped out by what he said. He presented me by going back to the day when I had asked him to go to lunch and telling his people, "I had already decided that morning that if nobody spoke to me, if I didn't make a friend that day, I was going to drop out of school. I was so lonely I couldn't stand it anymore." It still chokes me up to think that God can use ordinary people in such ordinary ways. Later, I got on my knees and thanked God that He had let me be there for Fred.

A friend is someone who walks in when everyone else has walked out. Onesiphorus and Titus and Onesimus were friends. They weren't theologically trained and hadn't gone to expensive seminars. But they knew how to be friends.

They remind me of a story I read about a young man who rode the el train in Chicago every day. If you have been on the el, you know that it passes very close to some apartment buildings. One day as the train slowed for a stop, the young man noticed a woman who was obviously sick in bed. Day after day he saw her looking out the window, and somehow found out her name and sent her a get-well card. A week later, when the train went by, he saw a big sign at the window saying, "God bless you! God bless you!" She didn't know his name because he had signed his card "the young man on the commuter train." But his reaching out to her had helped her to get well.

We can all reach out to one another. I was reminded of this when our daughter Cathy called me with concern about one of her twin daughters. Meg was practically running all over the house, but Jean was still crawling. I asked Cathy what Jean did when she saw Meg running so fast. "Daddy, she just sits there and claps." I told her, "Don't worry about Jean. Anyone who knows how to clap is going to be fine."

All of us are not equally gifted. God has, however, given most of us ability to clap and to encourage one another.

Helping Those Who Minister

David Livingstone's name is synonymous with the great continent of Africa. As a young man, Livingstone knew only that God had called him to service in Africa. He wanted to be a preacher. He gave his first sermon at a little church in Edinburgh. It was a disaster. In spite of all his preparation, he froze when he got in the pulpit and forgot everything he intended to say. After a long awkward pause, he managed to gasp—he was almost hyper-ventilating—that he had forgotten his sermon, and he walked out of the pulpit in shame and embarrassment.

A man by the name of Robert Moffett was there. He came up to Livingstone and said, "Young man, don't give up. You can be that servant of God He wants you to be. You can do it. He will help you. Why don't you become a doctor?" And so David Livingstone became a physician—and also a preacher. But where would he have been without Robert Moffett? Would there have been someone else to put fresh heart in him? I don't know, but I am thankful that Robert Moffett was there.

Do you remember the story about Paul in prison in Philippi when he and his companion sang praises to God and their chains fell off? Do you know the name of his friend? It was Silas. He was with Paul in the dungeon, and they had both been beaten. We don't have any sermons by Silas recorded for us in the Bible, but I'm glad he was there with Paul, one of those many saints in the shadows who make such a difference. When I was in Philippi I saw the Church of St. Silas and was glad that he has something for us to remember him by.

Every time you have a Livingstone, you have a Moffett.
Every time you have a Paul, you have a Silas, or Onesiphorus, or Titus, or Onesimus. Every time you have someone who does something great for the kingdom with fresh
heart—you also have a saint in the shadows who is putting
heart into them.

Everybody gets the mullygrubs. Everybody needs somebody. It was Aristotle who said, "You can't even tell the
truth if you don't have a friend." I know how true this is
because I'm the grateful recipient of encouragement from
people who brace me up day after day. I want to tell you
about some of them.

Cleve Ford was in his early seventies when I met him. I
went to be an assistant in the downtown Atlanta church
where he was a member. I was a student, and they let me
preach when I arrived and two years later when I left. Part
of my job was to go out visiting at night in Atlanta, and I
had never been in a big city before. I would knock on doors
and then give written reports of my visits. It was pretty
discouraging and awesome to me.

Cleve Ford understood that, so he gave himself to me,
adopted me, knowing what I was feeling. He said, "Bill, I'll
meet you down at the church. I'm retired now, and I'll just
go with you." Sometimes he would sit in the car and let
me make the visit, but he helped me with my map and my
flashlight to get out there and make the calls.

I remember the first time I went to see Miss Sadie. She
was a wonderful woman with a neurotic chihuahua. When I
sat down in her house, the little dog would be all over me,
would lick me in the face, sit on my lap, but when I stood
up to leave, he would try to bite me. He was a real mess.
Because Cleve didn't know about the dog, one night I took
him over to see Miss Sadie. We went in and sat down on
the sofa and visited and prayed with Miss Sadie. Then I
made as though I would stand up, but didn't. Cleve did, and

when he did, the dog took out after him. Of course, I eventually outgrew that kind of prank!

Every night—except that one after we were at Miss Sadie's—Cleve would say to me, "One day you're going to have your own church, and you're going to be a good pastor." He would believe in me and encourage me. After he died, his daughter took me by the hand and said, "Bill Hinson, my father loved you very much." I got a lump in my throat, and still do when I think about Cleve.

One day when I was visiting in the hospital, I got into an elevator with four people I didn't know. One of them was a man about eighty-five years old. As we started up, he said, "Do you know how long I've loved you?" I looked around to see who he was talking to, because I didn't grow up talking like that. He asked the question again, and I said, "Me?" and he said, "You. I've loved you for eight and one-half years, from the Sunday you arrived in Texas and preached your first sermon. I have prayed for you every day since then, and I prayed for you today."

I was just trying to get hold of that when the elevator stopped, and he and his daughter got off, and we started up again. Then the other couple said, "Yeah, and it's about time we told you how much your church means to our family too. Though we've never been there, we have listened to you year after year on television." And then they got off. You know, if it hadn't been for the ceiling in the elevator, I would have gone right on up by myself!

Those good words were like a tonic to me. And I have to remember that God has given all of us good words for other people. We all can brace each other up. We can be like a breath of fresh air for the people around us. We can be the tonic for what ails us—loneliness and discouragement.

Let's do it, for Christ's sake and in His name.

CHAPTER

Seven

The Real Work
of Parenting

The great King David sat between the inner and outer gates in the city of Mahanaim, where he had fled from his son Absalom. He sat in the place of judgment, and if the judgment of death had just been pronounced upon him, he could not have been in deeper distress. For King David was enduring those sleepless days and nights that every parent prays they will be spared . . . sitting and waiting for the inevitable word, the bad word of a son or daughter who has rebelled and gone wrong.

I wonder about David's reflections as he sat there with a watchman, looking for the runner who would bring word of Absalom and of the battle between his own army and that of his rebellious son.

I wonder if David thought about Maacah, Absalom's mother and one of his many wives. I wonder if he reflected on why he had married her. Maacah's father was Talmai, the king of Geshur, a neighboring state, and the marriage was probably contracted from political expediency.

I wonder if David thought about all the crises in the lives of Absalom and his beautiful sister, Tamar, and how he had neglected to take the responsibility of a father when they so much needed him to act. He must have remembered his eldest son, Amnon, who lusted after his half sister, Tamar, and how Amnon and his cousin Jonadab schemed to put Tamar into a situation where Amnon could rape her.

David's thoughts must have gone to Absalom's need for the king to bring resolution to this tragedy. When after two years David had done nothing, Absalom finally took the law into his own hands and killed Amnon for violating his sister. He then fled to Geshur to be with his grandfather.

I wonder if David remembered how his heart went out to his son during the three years he stayed in Geshur. He really did want a reconciliation with Absalom, but he never reached out to make it happen.

Joab, David's general and also his cousin, knew that the king was longing for Absalom, and so he sent a wise woman to tell David a story through which he saw himself and finally consented to let Absalom return to Jerusalem.

I wonder if David thought about his reasons for still not being reconciled with his son. Yes, he let him return, but only to his own house. David said to Joab, "he must not see my face." And so, for the next two years, Absalom, now a husband and father of four, lived in Jerusalem, but without seeing his father. At last, he sent for Joab and forced a confrontation with his father. When he approached the throne, Absalom "bowed down with his face to the ground before the king. And the king kissed Absalom" (2 Sam. 14:33). Seven years after the rape of his sister!

I wonder if David knew the extent of resentment which Absalom carried against him for his failure to behave as the father of the family. I wonder if he connected this rage to the uprising that was taking place, to the army that Absalom gathered around him. As far as Absalom was concerned, David was a "do-nothing king."

As David sat between the gates of Mahanaim, having been driven from home and humiliated, and having lost some of his closest supporters, his army and Absalom's were engaged to decide who would be the next king of Israel.

Yes, I wonder if David thought about what it means to be a parent. He had nineteen sons and one daughter who are named in the Bible, by an unknown number of wives. We read of eight, but he had nine sons by others. We can be sure he was aware of God's command that a king of Israel should "not take many wives, or his heart will be led astray" (Deut. 17:17). Still, I wonder if he ever thought about the real work of parenting, which is not just putting food on the table and clothes on the child, not just providing horses and chariots then—and cars now—and everything else the child wants.

I don't think David connected parenting with the formation of integrity in the child, or the formation of values, as we would say today. I doubt that he spent much time creating character in his children, and yet this is the real work of parenting, a work so important that we dare not trust it to another living soul. This is the responsibility of the two people who have joined with God in their creative process of bringing life into the world. And these two people are held singularly accountable for this real work of parenting.

The High Price of Success
As David sat between the gates, he and the watchman saw two runners approaching. The first man would not tell the

king that Absalom was dead; but the second, a Cushite, announced the good news of the victory. Then David asked if Absalom was safe. The Cushite blurted out, "May the enemies of my lord the king and all who rise up to harm you be like that young man" (2 Sam. 18:32).

David did not respond as the king, but as a father. "O my son Absalom! My son, my son Absalom! If only I had died instead of you—O Absalom, my son, my son!" (v. 33) We can feel the awful agony in these words. And yet we have to wonder about the outcome, had David responded as a father years earlier, instead of waiting until his son was dead.

David was a successful king. Israel had never had it as good as they did in the days of King David. But in his case, the cost of success was just too high.

Do you ever count the price of success in relation to your children? Do you ever consider the cost of being apart from them so many hours of the day and of the evening? Or, perhaps being gone so many weeks at a time? I have the feeling that if more parents really counted the cost, there wouldn't be so many daycare centers in America.

I know there are times and situations of need when both people have to work. I know how hard it is to buy a home. But I also believe that many people are seduced by Madison Avenue that tries to convince us of what the "good life" really is. Some people decide that to be "good" parents, they must give their children as much as possible. They sell out to materialism and then hide this sell-out behind a desire "to give their children the things they didn't have."

In the process, these parents fail to give their children the things they *did* have. They are defining inheritance as "that which you can spend, that which you can put in the bank." But that isn't the real inheritance we leave to our children.

Socrates once said that if he could find the highest place in Athens, he would cry to the people, "Why do you turn and scrape every stone to gather wealth and take such little care of your children to whom one day you will relinquish everything?" What he meant is that they were going to relinquish their wealth to people who didn't have the character even to know how to handle it. Instead of the wealth being a blessing in their lives, it would be a blight. Inheritance is much more than food and clothing and shelter; more even than costly tuitions and tennis lessons and expensive vacations.

What is the cost of success in your home? If you find it is too high, you could begin by looking for ways to simplify your life so that you will have more time together as a family.

You may have seen the "Hi and Lois" cartoon in which Ditto, their little boy, went to visit one of his rich young friends. The butler met him at the door and showed him to entire rooms filled with toys. Ditto said to his friend, "You and your daddy must have lots of fun playing with all these toys." The boy answered, "No, my daddy doesn't have time to play with me. He's at the office—he's got offices all over the world. He can't play with me." The little rich boy reflected for a moment and then said, "I guess that's the price of success."

When Ditto returned home, he threw himself into his father's arms and said, "O Daddy, I'm so glad you're not a success. I just couldn't afford for you to be a success!"

The Media Cannot Parent Your Child

Some people are so busy that they look to everyone else to instill values in their children. I'm sure David knew that Joab was trying to negotiate a reunion between Absalom and himself, but David never stirred. Maybe he just counted on Joab to work everything out between Absalom and himself.

There was a time when some parents counted on prayer in the schools to make their children Christian. There are people in this country right now who would tell you that the problem is that prayer was taken out of the schools. I don't like an educational system that excludes any mention of God either. But dear parents, the responsibility for making Christians of your children has never rested with the schools. I read about a little boy who came home with a terrible report card. When he saw the shocked look on his father's face, he said, "What can you expect, Dad? They won't let us pray anymore!"

Many people look to television to instill character in their children. It might be better said that they indiscriminately turn their children over to the television. Do you know that the only thing elementary-age children do more than watching television is sleeping? And do you realize that nonselective viewing means they are exposed to the most sordid elements in human personality day after day — elements you would never bring into your home?

Well-meaning parents who think they are so busy that they can't talk and do things with their children just turn them over to the idiot box. In the process, they are trashing their minds and trashing their souls. We become like what we take in all of the time. And that is particularly true of children. Adults can choose to reject certain influences, to be selective in what directs them. But children are so open, so naive, so innocent, and everything impacts them.

A high school boy had his heart set on the college of his choice. But he had not applied himself in the classroom and, as a result, the college turned him down. He went to his father and said, "Dad, I want you to pull some wires and get me into that college." His father said, "Son, what you really mean is that you want me to pull some *strings* for you. But, you said it right. You want me to pull some wires, and the first wire I'm going to pull is the television wire. And next I'll pull the stereo wire."

Did you ever listen to the words of hard rock? Some of it is obscene and pornographic. To let our children be subjected to it day after day is an effective way of saying, "I don't care about you. I'll feed you, clothe you, but I care nothing for your integrity, your values, or your character."

I really felt sorry for Noriega after he was detained in the American Embassy in Panama. They surrounded him with loudspeakers and played hard rock day after day, night after night. I never knew our country could be so cruel! To me that seemed like inhuman punishment.

The Wonderful Part of Parenting

The most wonderful part of parenting is to give our children what they need most from us—*ourselves*. A few years ago my wife gave me an exciting birthday gift, a new bicycle we named "Big Red Two." "Big Red One" wasn't nearly as shiny as this one. We bought it used when our children were little. It was a sturdy bike with balloon tires and it had a seat on the back, a basket on the front, and a thick handlebar. (We didn't know about the importance of safety helmets or child seats in those days.) I could put our smallest child in the basket, the next one on the back, and the oldest one on the handlebar and ride all three of them around the island where we lived.

After our children were grown and would all come home at Christmas and begin to talk about the good times they had had as children, they didn't mention about Dad buying them a car when they went off to college. They didn't even talk about college. When they thought about Dad in their younger years, they would mention "Big Red" and the times I would come home and call for them and we would set out on one of our island adventures.

Parenting means giving them yourself. The most valuable gift is to be with them, and for many parents today, that seems almost impossible, because they lead such hectic lives. If you are one of these parents, the Apostle Paul has a word for you. When he wrote his second letter to the church at Corinth, he mentioned several kinds of sins, such as "anger, factions, slander, gossip, arrogance, and *disorder*" (2 Cor. 12:20). Did you know that disorder is a sin?

There are families whose lives are so frazzled and disordered that they never sit down together around the dinner table. They never have a warm and friendly visit together. They never have devotions together. They leave messages on the refrigerator or the answering machine. They all sleep in their house, but they don't live together.

I consider the children of these families neglected children. Oh, they have plenty to eat, and they have more money in their pockets than we ever did at that age. But they are severely neglected.

If you don't have time to sit down and read the Bible with your children, you are too busy. If you can't begin the day or end dinner with a family devotion, if you can't choose some time in the day to be with your children, if you can't hear their concerns and then teach them how to pray for each other and for themselves, then you're too busy. And you are missing a glorious opportunity to do the real work of parenting. No one else is going to do it for you. And if you are not doing it, you are neglecting your children.

Casting a Long Shadow

Many of us have been blessed to have had a godly grandparent to be a light for us. My grandfather along with my mother gave me something money can't buy. The last time we went to Georgia, I drove 150 miles out of the way just to stand at Grandpa's grave. Do you have somebody like that? Every day my grandfather read at least one chapter from the Bible. Afterward, he would sing from the old shaped-note hymnal. People who learned to sing with the shaped notes did not need accompaniment. He and my grandmother sang when they were alone, and if the family was there, we were all invited to join them. It did not matter how many of us were there—when darkness began to fall, we knew it was time to gather in front of the fireplace in Grandfather's bedroom for evening devotions. Everything gave way to Bible reading, singing, and a prayer.

One of my very earliest memories about Grandfather's prayers was my need to get on the bed before he began to pray. I knew I would never make it through the prayer. I would always wake up the next morning knowing that I had gone to sleep and my father had carried me to my own bed. Later, I came to treasure those long but fervent prayers.

When my first son was about eighteen months old, he gave us a picture we treasure. My father-in-law and I had just come in from a hunting trip, and we were making ourselves comfortable in the den of the parsonage, waiting for supper to be ready. Just then, I saw John coming around the corner, sliding along in my boots, with his grandfather's hat on—and nothing else. This picture has always had a lodging place in my heart. John wanted to walk in his daddy's boots, and he wanted to wear his grandpa's hat.

Children are ever so susceptible to influence. This is why we are told that we must give account of every idle word spoken, and why there are such strong warnings against those who bring harm to the little ones. We need to be careful about those unguarded, offhand remarks, when we don't think anyone is listening. Children often are.

We all cast a shadow just by living, and as parents and grandparents, those shadows are especially long and influential. From them our children can take shade and comfort, but in them they can also be condemned to a dark place that is almost impossible to be free of. Those shadows we cast hold our values, our habits, our integrity or lack thereof, our goodness or badness, our love or hatefulness, our commitment to Jesus Christ or our commitment to ourselves. Everything we are lives in that long shadow we cast over those who come after us.

We have become used to hearing about the few ministers of the Gospel who bring shame on themselves. But the shadow cast by the clergy has been amazingly positive. It is said that there are more children of ministers and missionaries listed in *Who's Who in America* than of any other profession. The combination of faith and discipline and training and concern for other people has produced generations of clergy children who make significant contributions to the world.

Every so often we hear a parent say, "I don't want to influence my children about religion." Yet that parent is influencing his or her child about everything else. As parents, you can be sure that the world is influencing your children every day. You need to make up your mind whether you are going to be intentional in directing them in the right paths or whether you are really going to let them "decide for themselves when they are old enough."

In the Old Testament we find a tragic story about a family who seemed to have a hands-off policy when it came to training their children. The grandfather was Eli, the priest at Shiloh. You may remember him as the priest to whom Samuel's mother brought him as a child. Eli had two sons, Hophni and Phinehas, who had brought shame to the people of Israel. God had warned Eli about his sons, and He said to Samuel, "I told him that I would judge his family

92

forever because of the sin he knew about; his sons made themselves contemptible, and he failed to restrain them" (1 Sam. 3:13).

When the Philistines attacked the Israelites, they stole the ark of the covenant, and in the battle, Hophni and Phinehas were killed. Eli was sitting waiting for news, just as David had been waiting for news about Absalom. When the messenger came and told him that the army suffered heavy loss, that his two sons were dead, and that the ark of the covenant was captured, the old priest fell off his chair and died.

The wife of Phinehas was pregnant and near the time of delivery. When she heard the news of her husband and father-in-law, and about the ark, she went into labor and delivered a son, but the labor was too much for her. As she lay dying, the woman attending said, " 'Don't despair; you have given birth to a son.' But she did not respond or pay any attention. She named the boy Ichabod, saying, 'The glory has departed from Israel, for the ark of God has been captured' " (1 Sam. 4:20-22).

I know that oftentimes mothers and grandmothers make a heroic effort with children, even when fathers and grandfathers fail to be the influence they should. But sometimes that effort just isn't enough and parents know that they have an Ichabod. The glory is gone.

We need to be very intentional and very deliberate about what influences our children. We need to know the people who work with them in school and community, know who they play with, know what they watch and listen to and read, know where they go.

Do You Make Your Children Feel Special?

As parents we want to cast a shadow that blesses and does not blight our children, a shadow that heals and does not hurt. We need to stop looking for dramatic ways to cast a long shadow—when we become rich or famous. It is within the closeup and small things that we make the most lasting impression on the lives of our children.

I heard about a little girl who became ill and had to be hospitalized just prior to Christmas. When it became obvious that she would not be able to go home before Christmas, her caring and affluent family began to fill her room with expensive gifts. After a few days, her hospital room looked like a Toys R Us store. Her parents, meanwhile, continued to attend all their holiday social functions. Before they left her room each evening, they would always present her with another toy. One night when they gave her a toy and explained that they had to go out once more, she began to cry and held onto her mother. The mother asked, "What's wrong? Don't you like your new toy?" The little girl exclaimed, "Mommy, I don't want a new toy. I want you!"

One of my fondest memories of our children spans almost twenty years. When our three were small, my wife and I had a difficult time persuading them to eat breakfast. We thought that with a hearty breakfast, they would do better in school. In those days before we learned about high-fat content, we wanted them to have a substantial breakfast of bacon, eggs, pancakes, or the like.

Often I would cook breakfast while my wife got the children ready for school. I learned a secret about inducing them to eat pancakes. If I put the batter in a pitcher and then poured it out in the shape of the first letter of their names, they were so intrigued that they would eat every bite. When we had pancakes, I made a big "C" for Cathy, a "J" for John, and a "B" for Beth.

Years later, I had the joy of officiating at the marriages of our children. I also walked our daughters down the aisle and their mother gave them away. Every father who has ever escorted a daughter down the aisle knows how emotional that is. Just as I was about to walk Cathy down the aisle, she said something that really choked me up. She squeezed my arm and, looking up front toward the beautiful altar, she whispered to me, "All I'm seeing today is a capital 'C.'" It was almost too much for me!

How do you make your children feel special? How do you let them know how important they are to you? To God? To the church? It is in the little things we do and say, in those many small ways we give of ourselves, that we show just how precious our children are to us.

CHAPTER

Eight

Where Do I Find Meaning?

Dag Hammarskjöld, Secretary General of the United Nations in the 1950s, was a remarkable man who recorded his personal reflections in a book published after his death under the title *Markings*. In 1952, when he was at one of the lowest points of his life, he wrote, "What I ask for is absurd: that life shall have a meaning. What I strive for is impossible: that my life shall acquire a meaning. I dare not believe, I do not see how I shall ever be able to believe: that I am not alone."

Another writer of Hammarskjöld's generation, T.S. Eliot, wrote of the meaninglessness of life in the modern world, "We are the hollow men, we are the stuffed men, leaning together...."

Later, both Hammarskjöld and Eliot found a deep faith in

God through Jesus Christ, and wrote movingly of that certainty. But in their earlier searching, they expressed so well the feelings of emptiness that reach to our own times and are so evident in the music and entertainment as well as in the violence of our society. This empty feeling expresses itself in religion too, with new religions and remakes of old ones coming on the scene to tell us that they have the answer to the quest for meaning.

Jesus talked about this human emptiness, about the gnawing need people have in their souls for fullness. They are tired of holding on and want to be held. They have God in their mouths but want Him in their hearts. They may know Him as a memory of something they were taught, but they want Him as a present reality.

Evangelist Dwight L. Moody once held up an empty glass before an audience and asked, "How do I get the air out of the glass?" Someone said, "You get it out with a vacuum pump." Moody answered, "Oh, no. If you reach a perfect vacuum, the sides will cave in and the glass will break."

Then as the crowd watched closely, he picked up a pitcher and poured water into the glass until it ran over, and then said, "Now there is no more air in that glass." You don't dispel emptiness with more emptiness. Only fullness will satisfy.

If we are honest, some of us who are already Christians would have to confess that we have times when we don't feel as much meaning or fullness as we would like. Some of that may have to do with the pace and scatteredness of life today, with the way we work, with the loneliness that is so common in our society. And it may be that we need to make some changes in our lives.

But it may also be that we are ignoring the very resources that could make us feel satisfied and full and connected to ultimate meaning.

An Awful Wonder

When London's St. Paul's Cathedral was completed in 1710, Sir Christopher Wren, the architect of the monumental church, led Queen Anne on a personal tour. When they were finished, the Queen turned to Wren and said, "This sanctuary is amusing and awful." Today such a comment would be an insult, but in their day, amusing meant artful, and awful meant awe-full.

We have experienced a degeneration of language and, in the process, have lost the meaning of that little word *awe*. Today awful means unpleasant or terrible, not wonder-filled. And with the loss in our language, what has become of awe? What has become of the sense of wonder which has in the past marked the people of God? Someone has said that the secret of the early church is that they never got over the wonder of God's love in Jesus Christ and His church.

Such a sense of wonder is probably the most important part of our personalities and, if it is gone, we have lost one of our highest endowments from God. We see wonder as a natural expression from children, and we take it for granted in them. Unfortunately, most of us also seem to take for granted that we will lose a sense of awe as we mature. But this is not God's intention for us.

There is nothing we need today more than a sense of reverence. The Church of the Nativity in Bethlehem is constructed so as to make visitors kneel before they gain admittance into the sanctuary. It was probably built that way to keep horsemen from riding inside. The small, low door has stayed the same through the centuries, and is a good symbol for us. Many of the qualities and attributes of God are quite unknowable until we develop a sense of reverence. The world is full of burning bushes, but only those who see them will take off their shoes. The rest go on picking blackberries.

The city of Chicago has many public housing developments for poor people. Some years ago, members from an affluent church in the city bussed children from one of the housing projects to their sanctuary so that they might listen to an artist play their great organ. They believed that there was something in the human heart which might die if it was not fed with wonder. It was Einstein who said that if we have lost our capacity to wonder, we're dead already.

The emotion of the holy and the mystical is the most profound of all emotions, and yet so many people lack the sense of surprise at what God has done. Even in church we can say the words of our beliefs, can say the name Immanuel, God with us, and yet fail to wonder at the reality that God has visited us and continues to be with us. And if we are made so that we should experience wonder and awe, and yet don't, our sense of meaning in life is going to be skewed. For ultimate meaning is linked to reverence for the holy and to wonder in the presence of God.

In the Book of Genesis we read about Jacob who was running away from his parents' home after he had cheated his brother, Esau, out of his birthright. He had demonstrated that he was a crook, a cheat, and now he was fleeing from his brother's anger. On his first night away from home, he slept outside and dreamed of a wonderful ladder reaching to heaven on which angels were ascending and descending. As he watched this awe-filled sight, he heard a voice saying:

I am the Lord, the God of your father Abraham and the God of Isaac. I will give you and your descendants the land on which you are lying. Your descendants will be like the dust of the earth, and you will spread out to the west and to the east, to the north and to the south. All peoples on earth will be blessed through you and your offspring. I am with you and will watch over you wher-

102

ever you go, and I will bring you back to this land. I will not leave you until I have done what I have promised you (Gen. 28:13-15).

When the dream ended, Jacob awoke and thought, "Surely the Lord is in this place, and I was not aware of it" (v. 16). It isn't surprising that Jacob wasn't expecting God, after the way he had behaved; but, then, the grace of God has never been dependent on human behavior.

Jacob's second reaction was holy fear, and he said, "How awesome is this place! This is none other than the house of God; this is the gate of heaven" (v. 17). Jacob was expecting condemnation and judgment, and instead he received love and grace and a promise. He had met God and he renamed the place Bethel which means "house of God."

It was Cabot Lodge who said that if we have grown accustomed to something, we are already estranged from it—it is no longer ours. And Francis Bacon said that the only true atheism is to handle holy things without any feeling. Something has died inside our souls when we are no longer surprised and awed in the presence of God and His works.

The Apostle Paul wrote the Christians at Corinth that he had preached to them "in weakness and fear, and with much trembling" (1 Cor. 2:3). He had never gotten over the fact that the Lord had called him to preach, for he considered himself the chief of sinners. Paul had never gotten over the fact that after Christ had appeared to others, and then ascended to heaven, He appeared to him. He preached with an incredible sense of awe, for he knew that he was handling holy things.

Now and then the first people to shake my hand after the service say with surprise, "Why, your hands are cold." And I always say, almost under my breath, "It's because

I'm scared." I've been scared for thirty-two years, and if I ever get so that I'm no longer afraid, then someone should nail the lid on my coffin and carry me out and bury me. I'll be finished.

When we come to the place of meeting God, we are coming to the doorway of heaven. If any pastor can regard lightly the prospect of taking the hands of men and women and putting them into the hands of God, that person has lost the right to be a leader in the church of Jesus Christ. In fact, every Christian ought to be marked by a sense of awe about the church and its ministry. I am constantly reminded about the outreach of our own church in Houston and how many people are touched by its ministry. This is truly an extension of Christ in the world, as is every faithful church, for we are to continue to do the kinds of works Jesus did. This may mean planting churches in Russia or helping the homeless or ministering to people dying with AIDS. In whatever we do, we give to God our best, for our ministry comes from the awe-full wonder that God is working with His people.

The Bread of Life
Some people believe that Jesus' feeding of the 5,000 was His greatest miracle. Since the 5,000 numbered only the men, there may have been as many as 15,000 people who ate fish and bread from a boy's lunch. This miracle is recorded in all four of the Gospels.

However, there is more to the miracle than the dispensing of bread and fish. For one thing, the people knew from their Scriptures that the Messiah who would come would bring them manna from heaven, just as the Children of Israel had been fed manna in the wilderness. After He had fed them and the people kept following Him, Jesus accused them of coming after Him just so that He would feed them again. Some even tried to make Him king.

More than fifty verses in John 6 are devoted to the miracle of feeding and then a discussion between Jesus and the people about the meaning of the bread which comes down from heaven. When He told them that the bread of heaven gives life to the world, they asked, "Sir, from now on give us this bread." To this Jesus answered, "I am the bread of life. He who comes to Me will never go hungry, and he who believes in Me will never be thirsty" (John 6:34-35).

Jesus was not interested in feeding only the body. He was offering Himself as spiritual sustenance for people of all time. He knew that the bread that fed the body, necessary as it was, would satisfy for a short time. He was giving Himself as the bread that would nourish and fill people forever. He was asking them to invest their energies in the eternal.

You remember the prodigal son who wasted his living on his physical wants and needs. But he also had spiritual needs and finally found that he could not satisfy those by physical excess. When he was reduced to poverty, he realized that he could not feed his soul apart from reconciliation with his father. That part of him would be starved until he went home and repented. The same is true for us. Jesus promises satisfaction for those who truly come to Him. But the promise suggests that those who do not will never find the fullness of life that Jesus came to give us.

In one of his lectures, biblical archeologist James Fleming suggested that Jesus' declaration, "I am the bread of life," contains at least three meanings for us, as well as for the people of His time.

The first is a reminder of the mystery of God's work. Even with all that we know about agriculture, it still is a mystery that we can put a dried seed into the ground and water it and know that it will sprout and bring new life. We can reproduce all of the components of seed, but we still cannot find the life principle. We cannot understand how seeds found in the coffin of the Pharaoh in Egypt can sprout and grow after lying dormant thousands of years. Jesus told the people that God's work is that they should believe in the One God had sent. In other words, believing is God's work. Apart from the work of God in us, we can't explain why we believe; we can't even come to the point of believing unless God has first done His work of grace in us.

The second meaning is that bread is the very staff of life, the basic food of all peoples. And because of the place of bread and manna in the religious traditions of the Hebrew people, they broke bread together in a sacramental fashion. When Jesus broke bread with His disciples in the Upper Room, He gave this Passover bread a new significance. And when He broke the bread with the disciples on the road to Emmaus after His resurrection, they recognized Him in that moment.

The third meaning of the bread was tied in the Hebrew traditions to the making of a covenant. Beginning with Abraham, every time someone wanted to make a covenant, they would break bread together. A covenant held the element of mutual responsibilities and privileges, as well as protection for the weaker partner. The Jewish leaders of Jesus' time hated it that He ate with sinners, for they saw much more than just the sharing of food. He was offering them reconciliation.

During the Last Supper, Jesus offered bread to Judas, even when He knew that Judas was about to betray Him. He did it so that this Scripture could be fulfilled, "Even my close friend, whom I trusted, he who shared my bread, has lifted up his heel against me" (Ps. 41:9).

What does the last book in the Bible show Jesus doing? Standing at the door and knocking. "Here I am! I stand at the door and knock. If anyone hears My voice and opens the door, I will come in and eat with him, and he with Me" (Rev. 3:20). He is saying, "I will have a covenant of forgiveness and reconciliation." That's what the breaking of bread means in the Bible.

When Jesus had finished His declaration about being the Bread of Life, He said in effect, "If you will feed on Me, you will have eternal life, real life" (John 6:57). After this, many people drew away from Him. It was difficult for them to accept this, just as it is for us. For we are saved by the breaking of this bread. The only way we can receive Him is as broken bread.

There is a layman in a church in Houston who one day told his pastor how he came to be a Christian. He was spending his life in rebellion and disobedience to God. One day when he had been out doing all the wrong things, he came home and walked through the kitchen where his mother was working and on to his room. But just before going to sleep, he heard soft crying coming from the kitchen. He got up and tiptoed to the door of the kitchen. There he saw his mother kneading dough for the bread the family would eat the next day. As she was kneading, she was crying, and tears were falling into the dough. And she was praying over and over, "Lord, save my son. Help him to follow You."

The man returned to his bedroom and lay awake a long time. The next day he and the family ate the bread that his mother's love had made. When he ate it, he knew it was mixed with her tears, and this is what changed him forever.

It was Catherine of Siena, a fourteenth-century Italian saint, who wrote that Christ's divinity was kneaded into our humanity like one bread. And then that bread was broken for us, and the Holy Spirit serves it to us and asks us to receive it with thanksgiving and to let our lives be transformed by His gifts and graces.

Jesus promised that those who receive the Bread of Life will be raised up at the last day. I was reminded of this not long ago when I was called to an intensive care unit to see a woman who had been battling cancer and was now near the end. When I went into her room, I took her hand and squeezed it but she didn't respond. Then I called her name, and in a few seconds her eyes opened. When I said my name, I saw recognition in her eyes.

It was then that I thought about the last day of which Jesus spoke, and I shared this with her. I said that one of these days Jesus is going to do just what I had done. He is going to come to us when we are asleep, and He will call our name. He has promised to do this for everyone who has believed in Him as the Bread of Life, the source of the fullness of life, now and forever.

CHAPTER

Nine

"I'm Going Back to Church...Someday"

Likely every concerned lay person who reaches out to an unchurched person has heard the story. Pastors have it memorized and can tell it backward and forward. It goes like this, "I was once very active in church. I was there every time the doors opened. I gave my tithe, taught Sunday School, sang in the choir, ushered...." By this time we are wondering how they could have done all of these things.

When we ask where their church membership is now, they say, "Well, I think it is still in my last church, although it has been years since I was there. But I was baptized and was active in the church. I am a Christian. It doesn't matter that I'm not going to church, because I live for Jesus every day."

Long before the conversation ends, we know that we are getting an indefinite postponement. "Someday, I'll begin going to church again." When we ask about when "someday" is, they say, "I'm going to get back, but I can't be specific about the time." Indefinite postponement.

Important Family Responsibilities

Sometimes people will say, "I work all week and Sunday is the only day we have to be together as a family. After all, aren't we supposed to have one day of rest?" In reality, if Jesus had it right, Sunday is the only day we do not have. We have six days to labor and to do all those things we need to do, but on the Lord's Day we are to worship Him. When properly understood and enjoyed, worship is a source of energy, inspiration, and excitement.

I once heard Barbara Brokhoof, the United Methodist evangelist from Florida, tell how concerned her large family was because of her mother's exertion. Her mother worked incredibly hard all week at physical labor. On Sunday morning, however, she also got up early to make preparations for going to church. The family, fearing for her health, cautioned her about overexertion and advised her to stay home on Sundays and rest. Barbara said that her mother looked at them with unbelief on her face and inquired, "Don't you know it rests me to go to church?" This is a secret that many modern families have not discovered.

When we do discover the deeper meanings of worship, and especially the reality of the One whom we worship, going to church on Sunday is no longer a drag, but becomes the high-point of our week, for it energizes us for the days that follow. The problem, it seems to me, is in persuading some modern people to set their priorities in a way that will enable them to plumb the depth of meaning in Christian worship.

One day when Jesus was about to get into a boat to cross the lake, one of His many disciples came up to Him and said he would follow Jesus—but later. "Lord, first let me go and bury my father." Jesus replied, "Follow Me, and let the dead bury their own dead" (Matt. 8:21-22).

How could Jesus say something like that? After all, in the Old Testament, burying one's parents was a sacred responsibility given to the eldest son, and so this may well have been an eldest son speaking with Jesus. It is no accident that we take seriously the disposition of the remains of our deceased loved ones, for we have strong precedent in the Scriptures.

In the Book of Genesis we read the wonderful story of Joseph, then the ruler of Egypt, who had promised his father, Jacob, that he would bury him in the family plot in Hebron. When Jacob died, Joseph went to Pharaoh to request a leave of absence that he might bury his father. Pharaoh granted his request, and Pharaoh's officials accompanied Joseph on the trip.

When Joseph was approaching his own death, he asked his children and grandchildren to take his bones with them when the people of God left Egypt. It was 400 years later that the remains of Joseph went with the Children of Israel when they were delivered from the oppressive Pharaoh.

You may have seen the television series "Lonesome Dove" in which Gus exacted a promise from Captain Caw that if he died first, Captain Caw would bury him in the beautiful country we call Texas. When Gus died, it didn't matter that Captain Caw was way up in Montana. He fulfilled his promise. The last episode shows the struggle to return Gus' body to Texas. We do admire people who regard such promises as a sacred responsibility.

How then could Jesus, who also had sacred responsibilities, say such a harsh thing to this man—"Leave the dead to bury the dead"? To understand this, we have to know something about the customs of ancient Israel. People often spoke of fulfilling their family obligations by saying, "Let me bury my father." This was a figure of speech that meant, "Let me first take care of all my family responsibilities, and then I will do what you want."

We know this man wasn't speaking about an actual burial, because in those days they buried someone within twenty-four hours. The whole ceremony relating to the death of a parent didn't last a week.

This man was not willing to set a time; rather, he gave an indefinite postponement. And Jesus wasn't very gentle with him. He said, "I am Life, and I want you to belong to the Kingdom of Life. If you are separated from Me, you are spiritually dead. Now I want you to leave the spiritually dead to bury the spiritually dead, and come with Me to share the Gospel of Life."

The man didn't respond. We have reason to think that he was a religious man, for the disciple he was with was a teacher of the Law and called Jesus "Teacher." This man called Him "Lord." They are both called "disciples." And yet neither of them responded to Jesus. They both had more important things to do right then. Important family obligations, even religious obligations.

Counting on Spiritual Capital
This story we are examining has been called "the tragedy of the unseized moment." They were face to face with Jesus but did not have their affairs sufficiently in order to be able to leave and follow Him. They may have been very much like the former churchgoer mentioned earlier—looking at their past religious experience as a fire insurance. As a prepaid policy. They had spiritual capital and could respond to Jesus later, when it was more convenient.

Before the Reformation, the church had gotten into the business of selling merit. People could do good works or give specified amounts of money and purchase spiritual merit that would count later—in this life or the next. These good works would balance the bad, and the money the church took in would build new churches in Rome.

The people could even work for extra merit. This was called supererogation. If they felt a binge coming on, they could do a tremendous quantity of good works, and even after the binge was over, they would still come out ahead. They had spiritual capital! The word *supererogation* is one we need to take apart. *Erogation* looks similar to *arrogant* and really is. The Latin word *rogare* means "to ask." *Erogate* means "to claim or seize without justification or to claim on behalf of another." *Super* just increases the amount of the claim.

Supererogation was a form of indulgence that the church was selling in the time of Martin Luther, and was one of the reasons he finally knew that he had to stand against the authority of the Roman Church. He had come to understand that salvation was by grace alone, and that he could not purchase merit or grace or favor from God. There was no way to buy spiritual capital—with prayers or money or good works—or even with former church membership and good intentions about getting back to church someday.

Recently when a man was telling me his story about getting back to church "someday," I just couldn't help thinking about the cows on our farm when I was a boy. During the warm months, my father insisted that we periodically round up all the cows and put them through dipping vats to get rid of the ticks and other critters that bothered them so much. When this man was giving his excuses for not going to church—as if having been there long ago was going to take care of him forever—I thought of how we dipped those cows again and again. We didn't tell them that since they had been dipped once, there were

115

no more ticks in the woods, or that they now had tick capital.

There are still ticks in the woods. There is still spiritual conflict. There is still temptation. We know that we are not saved by having our name on a church roll or by being baptized. We remember Jesus' words in John 15 that tell us we are saved by our abiding in Him. "You abide in Me and I abide in you." Abiding isn't something you do once— like a cow going through a dipping vat—but something you do every day. Jesus was talking about the branch abiding in the vine, taking its life and nourishment from the vine. You know what happens to a branch that no longer takes life from the vine—it dies and you cut it off.

The man who wanted to bury his father may have missed getting on the boat with Jesus because he thought he had some spiritual capital left. Or, it might have been that he was trying to be humble, not wanting to ask too much. It has been years since I heard that old song "I just want a cabin in the corner of glory land." Don't talk to me about a mansion or a crown. I just want a cabin. I don't want a limousine—just give me a decal for my scooter windshield. I don't want very much—I'm willing to go economy class.

The only problem with this is that God doesn't have an economy class. Either you go first class or you don't go. First class is for people who love Him with their whole heart and soul and mind and strength. That is not second-class stuff.

Some of these people who think they will return to church "someday" are like the little boy who started buttoning his shirt wrong. His mother said, "Son, you are starting with the wrong button." He just went on buttoning and said, "It will come out all right in the end, Mom."

But it never does come out right in the end. People who

try to get everything straight in their lives before they accept a call to follow Jesus Christ never get it right. And those who one time heard the call but now think they can make it on their own don't get their lives buttoned up right either. The good news is that the church is waiting to welcome you. We know you aren't perfect, but then neither are we. If we were, we wouldn't let you in!

Not long ago, our church received a letter addressed to the First Methodist Church, Houston, Texas. No street address, no zip, but then our church has been in town for more than 150 years. The woman who wrote this letter was checking on one of her ancestors who had been a member of our church. She said, "I am writing to you and I don't even know if the church is still there." I wrote her back and said, "I have good news for you. The community of believers called First Methodist is still here."

The church will always be here. Why do you think those churches in Eastern Europe came out like spring flowers after the Iron Curtain fell? Why do you suppose that in Russia, where they were going to stamp out Christianity, people said that the church is the institution they most respect? Why do you think French theologian Theodore Béze said to the King of Navarre, "Sire, the church of Jesus Christ for which I speak has endured many blows and must not strike any. But I would remind you, sire, that the church is an anvil that has worn out many hammers." The church is the only permanent institution in the world.

There are two questions that people who have been long absent from the church will need to answer. The first one is, "When I get ready to return to church, will it be there?" Jesus has given a forever answer to that question, "Not even the forces of hell will ever destroy My church."

The second question is, "Will I get back to church? Am I any closer now than I was a week ago? A month ago? A year ago?"

117

The early church was impatient with procrastinators. That is why the Apostle Paul said, "Today is the time of God's favor, now is the day of salvation" (2 Cor. 6:2). And the writer of the Book of Hebrews said, "Today, if you hear His voice, do not harden your hearts. . . . Let us not give up meeting together, as some are in the habit of doing, but let us encourage one another—and all the more as you see the Day approaching" (3:15; 10:25).

Important Adult Responsibilities

When does someone become an adult? When I was young, teenagers raced their car engines and squealed their tires; they tried to inhale cigarette smoke without coughing and drink a six-pack at one sitting, and all sorts of silly things to prove they were grown-up! In our part of Georgia, when we could roll a barrel of turpentine up the skid poles and onto the back of the truck and head it up by ourselves, we were considered all grown-up. If we finished high school and if we went off and did two years in the army, we were for sure grown-up.

Today there are other ways in which young people try to show that they are adults. Illegal drugs is one example. Someone has said that taking drugs makes one feel as if he or she has just won a big race without having run it. It is a shortcut. Teenagers who take drugs feel as though they are adults. Becoming an adult, however, involves much more than just a feeling.

One of the surest marks of adulthood has always been the ability and the willingness to accept responsibility—for oneself and for other people. This kind of maturity doesn't come to us at a certain age. That is why some people are grown-up at sixteen and others are babies at fifty.

The Apostle John was the youngest of Jesus' disciples. Some think that he was only sixteen years old when Jesus called him to leave the fishing boats and follow Him. And this means that he was only nineteen when he stood with Mary, Jesus' mother, at the foot of the cross and heard Jesus ask him to take care of Mary. "Woman, behold your son." And to John, "Behold your mother."

Even as Jesus was attending to the redemption of the world, He felt responsibility for His mother, and He knew He could give her care to John. Of all the disciples, he was there, looking up into Jesus' face with a question, "What can I do for You, Lord?" Jesus had come into the world to establish a fellowship of the redeemed who have a common loyalty. This fellowship forms at the foot of the cross.

What does your life look like in terms of responsibility? Are you struggling for that beautiful balance that Jesus had, and which He wants all of His disciples to have?

Some people take more responsibility than they should and we call them neurotic. They make themselves miserable trying to make everyone else feel good. They can't say no, and so they take more and more responsibility — some of them even in the church.

On the other side, there are people who duck responsibility. Nothing is their fault. They never solve problems because they never take responsibility for them. These people feel quite happy, but they make other people miserable. They are a dead weight in any group they belong to.

We all need to strive for balance in our lives, to meet the many obligations that are truly ours. We live in a fast-paced world and constantly have to make choices about which responsibilities are really ours.

Important Community Responsibilities
The most recent Gallup Poll revealed that 56 percent of Americans are churched, meaning that they go to church at least once a month. We could quibble about what it means to be "churched" but that's their definition. The other 44 percent are unchurched, but almost half of them

119

say they believe in Jesus, and this would give you the idea that they did belong to the church at sometime. They just don't want to belong now.

Why do you suppose that is? Do you think that they don't know that the Christ they say they love has called them into fellowship in His body? Do you think it is because they have seen so many "hypocrites" in the church and they feel they are better than all those churchgoers?

I think one major reason is that the church is a community. The old Latin word for community meant "with wall." In our orientation classes for new members, I tell them that we are brought into this community by the action of God in the Holy Spirit. Once we are inside, we then are to take responsibility for that community by taking our places on the wall.

Do you remember the story of Nehemiah who led the Hebrew people in repairing the walls of Jerusalem? He divided the walls into sections and put families in charge of those sections. That meant that everybody was dependent on the other groups to keep the community strong. How do you keep the church community strong? Through your prayers, your presence, your gifts, and your service. If you identify with a church, they will expect you to do these things.

The people who don't want to identify with the church just don't want to get on the wall and be responsible for their part of it. They want the benefits of belief, but they don't want to take the obligations of belonging.

Life is a series of personal choices. We can choose to take responsibility or to ignore it. But having made our choices, we aren't victims. We are only experiencing the consequences of our choices.

Many of these people who were once in the church and are now absent are in the Baby Boomer generation, the ones who were called at a young age, like John was, but who then found that they had more important things to do. According to a recent survey of 400 people 34 to 42 years old, it isn't that they have any particular problem with the church, but that it doesn't "do anything for them." They are approaching it as consumers, or as employees buying into a benefit package but forgetting to realize that in buying or working, they have to put out to take in. In their "temporary" absence from church, they are making choices that could turn out to be permanent.

In the Atlanta area, everybody knew of Dr. Pierce Harris, the gravelly-voiced preacher at First Methodist Church. Dr. Harris went one day to preach at a penitentiary and an inmate asked for the privilege of introducing him. The introduction went like this: "Two boys grew up together. Both of them went to Sunday School, but one of them thought it was sissy and dropped out. The other boy stayed, accepted Jesus Christ as his personal Savior, and gave himself to serve Him.

"The boy who rejected Jesus Christ is introducing our speaker today. The one who accepted Him is the illustrious preacher before you."

We make our decisions—to be responsible or not to be. Then we live with the consequences. Jesus' confidence in the Apostle John was well placed. How about you? Is the confidence of Christ well placed in you? Can He count on you to do whatever He asks you to do?

CHAPTER

Ten

Who Says We
Can't Change?

In 1968, when our spacecraft *Apollo* was sending back pictures of the earth, we saw so clearly that small bluish ball we call home, drifting through space. But not everyone joined in applause for the mission. The Flat Earth Society attacked the pictures, saying they were fraudulent and a deceptive use of television cameras. They claimed that the earth is flat.

We smiled at the claims of this very small organization. But twenty-five years later, they are still growing and now have 1,500 members. They receive 3,000 letters each year from people who appreciate their work. Yes, we still smile when we hear about the Flat Earth Society because they seem to be going contrary to an overwhelming body of evidence in their resistance to change.

Yet, if we take such resistance to change out of the scientific and bring it into the spiritual, it doesn't seem as humorous. There is an enormously large Spiritual Flat Earth Society made up of people who say it is impossible to change. When that great preacher Wallace Hamilton heard someone say, "You can't change human nature," he responded, "There is more blasphemy in that statement than in a tent full of top sergeants!"

In recent years with the spread of the HIV virus, there has been so much discussion about prevention, and this discussion is always based on the way we view human nature. I heard one commentator say that he didn't know why we were surprised and shocked that public figures contract AIDS. He continued, "Humankind has been in this world for thousands of years. We aren't about to change now. Human nature doesn't change."

After hearing that Magic Johnson had the virus, a columnist wrote, "I suppose now, in light of what has happened to Magic, we are going to hear all kinds of hysterical calls for abstinence. But those calls will be largely wasted on our youth. Magic has chosen the practical approach belonging to the real world—safe sex."

When I read this, I thought that I must be one of those hysterical voices. I thought too about the implications of a study of high honor roll students in the United States. When these young people were asked about their attitudes toward drug use and premarital sex, most of them said that they didn't engage in either. If the call to abstinence is hysterical, it isn't wasted on the smart kids.

God was the original proponent of safe sex. Long before anyone else came up with the idea, God said that one man and one woman were to faithfully keep the marriage bed undefiled. That is safe sex! And if it is hysterical to talk about it that way, then I'll just have to be hysterical.

I agree that it is impossible to persuade or change people who measure life only by the physical and material, and who deny the spiritual. There is no way to convince them of the power that can change their lives. Yet, they can see the evidence of people around them who are faithful to one partner, even in the face of temptations. Why are these people so faithful to the highest and the holiest when they are surrounded by so much that is low and degrading?

I remember one handsome young man in his twenties who measured life by his new toys and his latest conquests. And I remember the wonderful day when he came to the altar of the church and accepted Christ as his personal Savior. Not long after that, he married. Fifteen years later, he and his wife have a strong marriage, and they are deeply involved in their church and community. When you ask this man why he is faithful, he has a simple response, "Jesus made me faithful and Jesus keeps me faithful."

The Spiritual Flat Earth Society
Jesus faced a Spiritual Flat Earth Society when He met up with a young man who had been born blind. Everyone knew him; he was a fixture in town. When Jesus and His disciples ran into the man, the disciples asked, "Rabbi, who sinned, this man or his parents, that he was born blind?" (John 9:1) There was a theory in those days that someone could be guilty of sin even before birth—we'd call that prenatal sin. Did he sin before he was born? Or did his parents do something awful? We know that God is a jealous God, visiting the iniquity of the fathers on the second and third and fourth generations.

Jesus didn't even try to answer these questions, because they were irrelevant. "Neither this man nor his parents sinned, but this happened so that the work of God might be displayed in his life" (9:3). The disciples were about to be in on an occasion of glory!

And so what did Jesus do next? He spit on the ground.

127

Today we don't like that word. When I was in grade school, we used to start fights about spitting. We would draw a line and then have two kids stand face to face and hold out their hands and say, "The best man spits on my hand." Of course, when one would spit, he would draw back his hand, and then there would be a fight. It was a fighting matter for someone to spit on another person.

But in the ancient world to which Jesus came, spittal was thought to have curative powers, and the spittal of a famous person was especially strong. In this situation, Jesus used a method familiar to the people, as He made a poultice from clay and put it on the blind man's eyes and then said, "Go, wash in the Pool of Siloam. . . . So the man went and washed, and came home seeing" (9:7).

This was news too good to keep in the neighborhood, and soon the whole town was excited about what had happened, and some of the local people decided that they should take the man to the Pharisees. Now, as you know, the Pharisees didn't like Jesus to begin with and and certainly didn't want news of this miracle to spread and enhance His popularity. When the Pharisees asked the man born blind how he had received his sight, he gave them a wonderfully simple answer: "He put mud on my eyes, and I washed, and now I see" (9:15).

To complicate matters, Jesus had performed His miracle on the Sabbath. To the Pharisees, making clay and putting it on the man's eyes was work, and this proved to them that Jesus could not have come from God, for He was not keeping the Sabbath. The logical question from some bystanders was, "Well, how could a sinner do such miraculous signs?" And so the argument continued.

Finally the Pharisees turned again to the young man who had been listening to all the debate and asked, "What have you to say about Him? It was your eyes He opened" (9:17). When he said that Jesus was a prophet, the Jews ignored him and sent for his parents. There must be some trickery going on, they concluded; he couldn't have been born blind. Maybe he had a twin.

Sounds like a Spiritual Flat Earth Society to me. They see someone get healed of body or mind or soul; they see someone get converted, and they can't believe he is the same person and have to check it out with his family. The Pharisees asked the parents, "Is this your son? Is this the one you say was born blind? How is it that now he can see?" (9:19)

Because the parents were afraid of the synagogue rulers, they didn't want to give a direct answer, and so they said, "We know he is our son, and we know he was born blind. But how he can see now, or who opened his eyes, we don't know. Ask him. He is of age; he will speak for himself" (vv. 20-21).

The Doubters

The man's neighbors also offered an interesting commentary on what had happened. Some claimed he was the same man who used to sit and beg, but others said, "No, he only looks like him." He was the same and yet he wasn't.

This reminds me of going back to preach in my hometown. It was twenty years after I graduated from high school in Hazelhurst, Georgia that I went back to preach in a revival campaign. During the first service, I saw a woman staring at me the whole time. After the meeting she had one question for me, "Are you ... you aren't ... ah ... Charlie Hinson's boy, are you?" I said I was. "Really, you aren't Charlie Hinson's boy, are you? Not the one who was in those terrible fights at the football games and all? You aren't Charlie Hinson's boy, are you?" I said I was.

I am, but I'm not. This is he, the people said about the man born blind, this is like him. When Augustine was converted, he walked down the street one day, and a former mistress called out to him. He kept on walking as if he hadn't heard her, and so she came closer and said, "It is I, it is I." But Augustine responded, "Ah, but it is not I." "This is he." "This is like him." Some people just can't handle such tremendous change. If they can't measure it in a test tube, if they can't get hold of it in a physical way, they just won't buy it.

The man born blind was no theologian, but he knew what had happened to him. The religious experts grilled him, and what he had to say to them came down to this, "I don't know much about Jesus. But one thing I do know—I was blind but now I can see!"

This story makes me think about Joe Sardler who had been blind for six years because of atrophy of the optical nerve. One night he tripped over the dog's dish and fell down the basement stairs. As he fell, his head slammed against the wall—and suddenly Joe could see. He kept his family up the whole night as he looked at things he had missed for so many years, including his five-year-old daughter.

People kept saying to him, "How did it happen, Joe?" He told them God did it. God used the dog dish and the basement stairs and the wall. Joe gave God credit for the miracle.

The man Jesus healed had faith, but the Pharisees who were quizzing him didn't *want* to believe. Some people are that way. They just love to hear about a TV evangelist gone bad, or about a backslidden preacher, or a sour saint with a shriveled soul. Such news reinforces their belief that the change these people claimed wasn't really so in the first place. You see, if these doubters really believed that Jesus could change people, *they* would have to change.

These skeptics want to see finished Christians, and there aren't any around. But there are lots of unfinished ones. Even the saintly Howard Thurman said that parts of him had never yet heard the Gospel. Charles Wesley prayed, "Finish then Thy new creation." None of us can claim to be finished. But that doesn't refute our testimony—once we were blind but now we can see!

The Sleepers

Some members of the Spiritual Flat Earth Society fail to understand the reality of change because they are asleep spiritually. They are like the foolish maidens in Jesus' story who failed to get the oil they needed for when the bridegroom would arrive. When he did come, they awoke and asked the wise maidens to give them some. But they were told, "No, you must buy your own."

No one else can give you the spiritual preparation you need. Yes, people can pray for you, but they can't pray your prayers. They can have faith that you will believe, but they can't exercise your faith. Either you have made that preparation or you haven't.

The Bible indicates that the natural state of human beings is spiritual deadness or asleepness. God told Adam, "If you disobey Me, and eat of this forbidden fruit, you will surely die." The serpent had said, "You will not die." And, as a matter of fact, Adam kept on walking around. But did that mean that he didn't die? Of course not. He died spiritually. When God says that the soul that sins shall surely die, He means precisely that. When we willfully and deliberately continue to sin against God, we die spiritually. Jesus talked about people who don't have ears to hear or eyes to see. A kind of blindness comes over them. Because they do not know the nature of their malady, they don't have a clue as to its remedy. They feel no sense of need for God. They are asleep in their deadness and have a false sense of peace. They don't conquer sin—they don't even fight against it. They have no problem with temptation because they give in to it. They need to be spiritually awakened. They need to undergo a radical change.

When the Spirit of God awakens people, they first struggle against sin, and then come to the realization that they cannot defeat the sin by themselves. The sin defeats them, and they feel like Br'er Rabbit fighting Tar Baby. They are stuck to the sin. No matter what they do, they lose until they turn to God.

The person who is spiritually asleep has false peace. The person who has been awakened has no peace—and just enough religion to make him miserable. There has to be something more. The Apostle Paul said, "Wake up, O sleeper, rise from the dead, and Christ will shine on you" (Eph. 5:14).

Of his conversion experience, Charles Wesley said, "When it pleased God to open my eyes. . . ." The first time he really saw his need, he cried out, "O Lord, have mercy on me, a sinner. I need You, Lord." He cried and prayed until the Lord God of heaven heard and came and forgave his iniquities and filled him with His presence. Comparing his life before and after conversion, Wesley said, "Before, I fought and was always conquered. Now, with Christ in me, I am always the conqueror." That is the good news of the Gospel.

Celebration for the Changed

There will come a day when the only show in town is to serve God day and night. How do you feel about that? The way you answer will tell you a lot about whether you have been changed, transformed, in the way that God desires for you.

In the Book of Revelation (7:9-17), the vision the Apostle John saw as an old man, there is a powerful scene in which a multitude of people are standing before the throne of God. It is a multitude so large that no one can number them, and it represents all the tribes and nations and languages on earth. This is a diverse group and illustrates that heaven is not going to be a homogenized blend where everyone is alike.

But there is one thing that they all do have in common—they are all wearing white robes which speak of the victory they have won over sin in Jesus Christ. They are all clean. Those robes have been washed in the blood of the Lamb, and that phrase speaks of the self-emptying love of Jesus Christ. It is through the once-offered sacrifice of the Lamb, Jesus, that our sins can be forgiven.

To be part of this white-robed multitude is to have the ultimate proof of the transformation that God begins and completes in those who come to Him in faith. The old hymn that comes from this scene asks, "Are you washed in the blood of the Lamb?" It is not, "Have you made a good impression?" or "Are you smart enough?" or "Do you have a high profile?" but, "Have you come clean with God?"

In our culture we hear so much about being OK and about God accepting everybody. It is true that God loves everyone, but He wants us to be transformed, changed new creations in Christ.

Jesus met the woman who was caught in the act of adultery when some people threw her down at His feet, hoping He would order her stoned (John 8:2-11). When He said that the one without sin should throw the first stone, they all left because they could not in honesty condemn her. Then Jesus said to her, "I don't condemn you either." But He added something very important. "Don't sin anymore."

Jesus always lifted people. He always called for a transformation of life. Any person who is in Christ is a new creation. Acceptance, brilliance, and high visibility will never replace being washed in the blood of the Lamb.

The greatest need of every person is to come to God. The most basic need is to be made clean by Christ. It doesn't matter that you have tried everything else to find satisfaction and peace. Jesus said, "The one who comes to Me I will not cast out.... Come to Me, all who labor and are heavy laden.... Come, everyone who has a stain."

Notice that the verse says, "They washed their robes." There is a part for us to play—to acknowledge our need of Him, to come clean, and give Him a chance to change us.

Who says we can't change?

CHAPTER

Eleven

Connecting Faith
and Finances

We don't really know God until we know Him financially. It is a poor faith that has no connections to the financial part of our lives. The Scripture plainly teaches us that we are to honor the Lord with our substance, and each time we follow that practice, we are making a declaration that our trust is in God. We are saying that as God's people we look to Him for all the good gifts of life.

Now sometimes we forget that God is the giver and think that our own cleverness has gotten us all that we possess. I am reminded of this when I have a bad throat, for what is a preacher without his voice? I have preached with a sore throat more times than I can remember, but once in a while I am left without any voice at all. And when that happens, I remember that every gift we have—physical, material, spiritual—comes from God. We hold it all in trust, as a treasure from Him.

When we talk about honoring God with our substance, with all that we possess, we are talking about a basic test of authentic faith, for giving is at the heart of what it means to be a Christian.

A story is told of three boys who were deciding what they wanted their father to leave to them when he died. The oldest boy said, "When Dad dies, I want him to leave me his watch. I've always admired it." The second boy said, "Well, I'd like for him to leave me his ring—I've always loved that ring." And then the youngest one said, "I want Dad to leave me all of his canceled checks." His older brother asked in surprise, "Why do you want his checks? They aren't worth anything." And the youngest boy answered, "I want them because Grandpa says that if you look at a person's canceled checks, you can learn all there is about him. I want to know everything about my father."

One of the most revealing objects any of us has is our checkbook—and then the canceled checks which follow. In fact, we can learn a great deal about ourselves by watching how we spend our money. We can trace our priorities by the checks we write. We can see how well we are honoring God with our substance, as well as meeting our other obligations.

God Wants a Tithe
The Bible is very specific when it tells us to honor God with our substance. We are to give a tithe. There seems to be some confusion about what this means, especially for the dollar-dropper who will say, "There's my tithe." He placed a gift in the offering, but I doubt that it was a tithe, unless he's unemployed.

A tithe is 10 percent of your income. This is an ancient formula that we read of very early in the Bible, when the patriarch Abraham offered a tithe to Melchizedek who was king and priest of Salem. We read about this man again in the New Testament Book of Hebrews, chapters 5–7, where the writer quotes Psalm 110:4, "You are a priest forever, in the order of Melchizedek," and then shows that these words refer to Jesus. "He has become a high priest forever, in the order of Melchizedek" (Heb. 6:20). Though this section in Hebrews is talking about the whole matter of the priesthood as it relates to our eternal salvation, it is also significant for us to think of Jesus as the one to whom we pay our tithes, just as Abraham paid his to Melchizedek in his day and received a blessing from him.

From Abraham's time, we can follow the standard of the tithe right through the Bible. The Prophet Malachi delivered God's message to the people of his time:

"Return to Me, and I will return to you," says the Lord Almighty.
"But you ask, 'How are we to return?'
"Will a man rob God? Yet you rob Me.
"But you ask, 'How do we rob You?'
"In tithes and offerings. You are under a curse—the whole nation of you—because you are robbing Me. Bring the whole tithe into the storehouse, that there may be food in My house. Test Me in this," says the Lord Almighty, "and see if I will not throw open the floodgates of heaven and pour out so much blessing that you will not have room enough for it" (Mal. 3:7-10).

In Matthew 23:23 we read of an encounter Jesus had with the legalistic scribes and Pharisees, in which He endorsed the ancient formula for giving a tenth of one's income. He said to them:

139

You hypocrites! You give a tenth of your spices—mint, dill, and cummin. But you have neglected the more important matters of the law—justice, mercy, and faithfulness. You should have practiced the latter, without neglecting the former.

The Apostle Paul wrote to the Corinthian church about an offering for Christians who were in need. He said, "Do what I told the Galatian churches to do. On the first day of every week, each one of you should set aside a sum of money in keeping with his income . . ." (1 Cor. 16:1-2). God is infinitely fair. Someone called me recently and said, "Pastor, I'm not making a nickel. How can I give?" I said, "Ten percent of nothing is nothing, my friend. This is a time for you to let the church minister to you." God says that we are to give according as the Lord has prospered us.

Trusting God with the Tithe
A young couple in a church I pastored learned a lesson about tithing. Prior to coming to Christ, they had made large amounts of money, and then their fortunes reversed and they lost much of it. So this couple succumbed to the temptation to squirrel away some of their cash in a safety deposit box. They were afraid that they might go bankrupt and thought that at least they would have something. Over several years, they accumulated a very tidy nest egg, knowing that if they did have to declare bankruptcy, no one would know about the savings.

I found out about this when the husband came to my study and dropped a bundle of $100 bills on my desk. It was a tithe of the money they had put in the safety deposit box. He and his wife had had a new experience of the grace of God, the love of God, and some things started happening inside of them to prove that the change was real. He told me, "I had to do this, because putting that money away

140

was not honest. I want the church to have a tithe, and then I'm going to declare the rest of it to the IRS. If I go bankrupt, I go bankrupt. If I lose everything, I lose everything. But now I have Jesus Christ, and in Him I have everything."

This man and his wife had discovered that they could trust God for transient matters. Have you made that same discovery? You trust Him for eternal things, you give Him your life, so you surely can trust Him for food and clothing and shelter. When Jesus spoke to the multitude in what we call the Sermon on the Mount, He said:

Do not worry about your life, what you will eat or drink; or about your body, what you will wear. Is not life more important than food, and the body more important than clothes? Look at the birds of the air; they do not sow or reap or store away in barns, and yet your Heavenly Father feeds them. Are you not much more valuable than they? Who of you by worrying can add a single hour to his life? (Matt. 6:25-27)

Honoring God with the First Fruits

On a visit to Israel, our group was taken to the ruins of the ancient town of Chorazin, which was near Capernaum. Chorazin was on the northeast side of the Sea of Galilee, up in the hills that covered volcanic rock. Because of eruptions in the past, the earth covering the volcanic rock was warm, and this warmth meant that spring crops could be planted there earlier than in other areas. This meant too that the crops in Chorazin were the first to be harvested in the fall. There were designated runners, people who would go to Jerusalem to offer the first fruits of the harvest before the altar of the Lord.

I found this an intriguing picture, especially as we think of tithing. For it is precisely at the point of the first fruits

141

that many people have made their mistake in their attempts to tithe. Giving of the first fruits means taking it off the top. But so many people think that they can first cover all their expenses and desires, and then if something is left over, they'll give it to God. That's like starting to button your shirt at the wrong hole. It won't come out right. When you take this approach, you are going to have trouble with your finances. When you honor God with your first fruits, He will help you with your total financial management. I am convinced that the finest managers of money I have ever known in my thirty years of ministry are the long-term tithers. I remember the first Sunday night at my first parish. After the service, some of us were standing around talking, like so many people do on Sunday evenings, when they aren't in a hurry. A prominent member who had his own accounting firm, and was also very generous to the church, was talking to me when an elderly man shuffled past us. The businessman said to me, "You don't know it now, but there goes the greatest giver in this church." I was intrigued by his comment, because the man next to me was very generous. But he pointed to the elderly man who didn't look prosperous at all and said he was the greatest giver.

Some time later, the elderly man, whose name was Mr. Cooper, became ill and I went to see him. He lived in a housing project, where residents had to prove their poverty to get an apartment. It was a winter day, and we sat near a kerosene heater trying to keep warm as we talked. I learned some things about him that day—that he had an income of $35 a week, and that he drove an old Plymouth he had painted over and over again. He couldn't afford a good paint job, but just kept applying the paint himself to the bad spots. I learned too that he always carried with him a little notebook in which he would record the date and the amount when he gave his tithe to the Lord. And sure enough, when he got back to church, I could see him taking out the notebook after the offering and recording the date and the amount. In the four years that I was privileged to be Mr. Cooper's pastor, I came to understand what the affluent member had said about his being our greatest giver.

Most of us earn more than $35 a week. But regardless of how much we earn or have, I am convinced that when we honor God with a tithe, the 90 percent goes further. It has more stretch to it. There is more bang for the buck. And something else happens too—there is more quality in the way we live. Life goes better when we keep our eyes on eternity. In the blessing of tithing we learn not to get caught up totally in the now, but to keep our eyes on what is coming.

Treasures in Heaven
Jesus told us to lay up treasures in heaven. I was reminded of this one morning when I arrived at church and our receptionist told me about a man who had come in looking for a copy of the devotional booklet *Upper Room*. He didn't have any money and wanted to give us something in exchange for the booklet, and insisted on leaving a food stamp. As I looked at that stamp, I realized anew that there is something more basic than bread. Our relationship with God stretches all the way through this world right on into the next. We have a little while in this life, and then very quickly we are with our loved ones in the world to come. Jesus said, "Do not store up for yourselves treasures on earth, where moth and rust destroy, and where thieves break in and steal" (Matt. 6:19). In His day, much wealth was invested in fine garments. To have moths was a disaster. Rust speaks of something that eats away treasure, whether metal, or a barn full of grain that rats and mice destroy. Thieves broke in and stole then, as they do now.

Nothing material is sacred or permanent.

When we were in the Middle East, we saw the pyramids of Egypt that were built almost 3,000 years ago, to preserve the treasures of the kings and nobles. But often, before the mourning was over, grave robbers had broken in and walked off with the treasure.

Thieves do break in and steal. Jesus said, "Don't trust your life to that which the years or thieves can take away. Don't give your highest affections to what can be lost in this world. Lay up treasures in heaven."

God Is So Good

When we lose sight of our dual citizenship—this world and the next—we become, in the words of G.K. Chesterton, "blind to our larger blessings." We thank God for presents in our stockings; but, as Chesterton reminds us, we ought to be thanking God for legs to put in our stockings.

I was reminded of a larger blessing recently. I came home from work one day and found my wife baby-sitting our two grandchildren who live in Houston. The older is nearly three, and the younger almost two. Needless to say, our house was showing the strain of two toddlers having been there for five hours. Jean was sitting in the middle of our bedroom floor, with toys scattered all around and the children climbing on their grandmother.

As I entered the room, she looked up at me with eyes full of tears, and I realized that I had happened on her and the children at a very special moment. As Jean reached out to caress the children, she said to me, "Isn't God good? Isn't God good?" And suddenly I had to leave the room, because a flood of emotions made me lose my voice.

Several years ago, my wife had breast cancer, and we were unsure about the prognosis. One of the first things she said to me in the middle of the trauma of the surgeries that followed was, "I won't live to see my grandchildren."

144

She had never said that again, but when she looked up at me that afternoon and said, "Isn't God good?" the recollection of her statement about the grandchildren hit me like a ton of bricks.

God is so good! He's so good to me and to you. When we keep our loyalties to heaven intact, we will not lose sight of God's matchless mercies here below.

As we live in a constant state of gratitude, we find it easy to give, for it is one of our greatest joys. And then, even if our prayers aren't answered as we requested, we know God's grace to be sufficient.

CHAPTER

Twelve

Values? Or Transforming Power?

I am bothered by all the talk about values. That may sound strange, coming from a Christian minister. Certainly I believe values are important, but I believe even more in redemption. When the talk about values means just adding a package of good behavior to make the person more respectable, redemption seems beside the point. Jesus is not in the business of patching up people, but of redeeming them.

Before the Apostle Paul was converted, he had values. As Saul, he was a Pharisee of the Pharisees. And yet he rattled on the inside like a marble in a metal can. He was empty. He kept the entire law, and he was angry because it didn't profit him at all.

If all we need is values, then we don't need Mount

Calvary; Mount Sinai is enough. We don't need grace; the Law is enough.

Before my wife and I moved to Houston, burglars broke into our home and took some sterling silver that had been in our family for generations. The insurance company replaced it, insofar as you can replace silver that has cherished initials of family members long since deceased. On the day after we bought new silver, we discovered that the burglars had entered once more and stolen our replacement silver even before we had put it away.

Our sense of indignation and of being violated is a feeling well known to many Americans. It is a sense of rage that goes unventilated because all too often the culprits go unpunished, or engage in some legal delaying tactics that rarely result in real justice.

We are surrounded by crime today. People are beaten and robbed with regularity. One of our church members had her home burglarized and then burned for vindictive good measure. Especially in our cities, people are killed every day, and we almost seem under siege because of the prevalence of crime. We would feel a sense of satisfaction if we could put the criminals away somewhere and lose the key. They just have no values!

How Are People Changed?

Yet, in our more thoughtful moments, we recognize that we cannot depend upon the force of law and the fear of punishment to correct the deepest ills of society. The problem is deeper than this. The Apostle Paul acknowledged it when he said that he saw another law at work in himself. He recognized cross-purposes in his life that led him to do things he didn't want to do.

When we consider our contemporary problems in this light, we realize that many of our modern solutions respond to the symptoms but leave the actual problems untouched. Whether the problem is outright crime or low morals, we cannot hope to change people by laws and by moralizing.

A while ago, I saw a movie about the Civil War, "Glory," that was set on the Isle of Hope in southeast Georgia. The movie was about the 54th company which was composed mostly of runaway slaves who wanted to be part of the Union Army. They had been trained by a white colonel, but they didn't have adequate clothing or arms and were not allowed to fight at first. In frustration, one young soldier ran away. He was caught and about to be publicly flogged. He was made to hold onto a wagon wheel in a spread-eagle position as his shirt was jerked off his back.

The colonel, who was present for the beating, knew that he was defeated when he saw the man's back. It was ribboned with scars from previous beatings. There was defiance in his eyes as he fixed them on the colonel. He did not cry or wince as the whip was laid to his back, but the colonel showed his distress. Although he didn't touch the young man, he had ordered the beating.

Later, when the colonel asked the soldier, "Would you like to carry the colors of the company?" he answered, "Colonel, I'll never carry your colors!"

After they won the right to fight, something happened in a battle to change the young man. In the last charge, the colonel ran out in front of his men and up the side of a hill and was cut down by a hail of bullets. As the young soldier saw his colonel die, he jumped to his feet and picked up the colors and joined the officer in death. What changed him?

What changed Simon Peter after he denied his Lord, cursed, and said he had never known Him? He looked into the eyes of a gentle Lord who didn't backhand him and tell him how ungrateful he was. Rather, Jesus loved him and offered him grace.

What changed Saul to Paul? A life-changing encounter with the living Lord whom he was persecuting, as he harassed the Christians.

In our society, we desperately need something that is beyond human ability. Our greatest need is for transformation of heart and life. That comes through God's work of conversion in the individual, and for that we must depend on God. How does it happen? It begins when we realize that we can't do it, that there is something in us we just can't wrestle down. With Paul, we confess, "I have the desire to do what is good, but I cannot carry it out. . . . When I want to do good, evil is right there with me" (Rom. 7:18, 21).

This kind of honest humility isn't easy, but it is necessary before anything of significance can happen in our lives. I am reminded of a businessman who was very overweight. One day at work he announced that he was going to lose those unwanted pounds. And yet, the next morning he walked into the office carrying a gigantic coffee cake. His staff asked him, "What's going on?"

He said, "Let me tell you. On my way to work this morning, I passed a bakery and saw this coffee cake in the window. I don't think it was there by accident. So I prayed, 'Lord, if You want me to have that coffee cake, let there be a parking place right in front of the bakery.' And sure enough, on the eighth time around the block, there it was!"

Sometimes the only thing that keeps people from starting on the road to conversion is a lack of honesty. They haven't gotten to the point where they are willing to level with God and say, "I can't." And so they try values. Or religion.

I don't call people to be faithful to religion, but to receive a faith that will save them from a dead religion. I want them to admit, "I can't," and then to say with Paul, "But God can." Look at what he said:

In my inner being I delight in God's law; but I see another law at work in the members of my body, waging war against the law of my mind and making me a prisoner of the law of sin at work within my members. What a wretched man I am! Who will rescue me from this body of death? Thanks be to God—through Jesus Christ our Lord! (Rom. 7:23-25)

If you have been pursuing religion or values but not the Savior, give Him permission to transform you. Yes, you do have to give that permission. God is going to let you pull your own wagon as long as you say, "I can handle it."

My friend Monty was a chain-smoker for twenty years. He lit one cigarette with the one he was smoking and would even wake up in the night and smoke. It was killing him. We prayed for Monty and with him about this, because he wanted to quit but just couldn't. Finally, one day he faced the reality of what was happening in his life. He had just started to break open a fresh carton when he met the Lord and fell on his knees and said, "Lord, I can't do it. Will You help me?" It was twenty-one years later that he told me, "I've never even had the desire to smoke again."

How Is the Church Changed?

The church is changed as individuals are changed. Before the Resurrection, Peter denied Jesus. But not many weeks later, Peter and John healed a crippled man and then told the watching crowd, "You disowned the Holy and Righteous One . . . You killed the Author of life, but God raised Him from the dead. We are witnesses of this. By faith in the name of Jesus, this man whom you see and know was made strong" (Acts 3:14-16).

This stirred such a commotion in Jerusalem that the authorities feared for their influence in the community. They sent for Peter and John, planning to bring them be-

153

fore the Council and embarrass them enough that they would go away. They knew that the two were uneducated men, and they thought, "We can intimidate them." So they hauled them before the Council. They asked their most learned questions, thinking surely the disciples would stumble in their defense. But instead, they spoke with such boldness and straightforward simplicity that the judges called a five-minute recess to figure out what went wrong.

They said, "Our strategy has backfired. Instead of embarrassing them, we have only given them a forum for the advancement of their faith. What has happened to them? How can they be so bold? *They must have been with Jesus.*"

This is what will change the church. This is what the world wants from us. I believe the world is waiting to see Christians whom God has touched. Just to be around such people is to know that Christ has touched their lives. *They must have been with Jesus!*

In my denomination, we claim the heritage we have received from John Wesley. However, he lived through years of frustration and anxiety as a pastor and a missionary before he was touched by Jesus. It was at a meeting on Aldersgate Street in London, where someone was reading from Luther's Commentary on the Book of Romans, that Wesley's heart was "strangely warmed." And from this heartwarming experience, Wesley transformed the face of Christendom in Britain.

Although John Wesley was a scholarly man, and although this Aldersgate experience included knowledge, it was far more than that. From that day on, Wesley was a man of the trained mind *and* the warm heart, of intellect *and* vital piety. For all his learning, his experience with Christ was always primary for him personally, and this was evident in his message for the thousands to whom he preached, most of whom were untrained people.

I had a running controversy some years ago with a seminary professor who didn't believe Jesus was the Son of God. To let him teach in a seminary is worse than letting a butcher teach surgery in a school of medicine. In the midst of our struggle, I said that, although he was a great technician in terms of knowing the mechanics of the New Testament languages, he still didn't know the New Testament. He didn't know the One the New Testament was written to reveal, and that left him illiterate as far as the Christian faith was concerned.

In those ghastly days after the bombing of our Embassy in Lebanon, we watched with horror as mangled bodies of our men were pulled from the wreckage. One marine was mutilated beyond belief; he had concrete splinters in his eyes as a result of the explosion, and his head was completely wrapped in bandages. When his commander went to visit him, he saw more tubes going in and out of the marine's body than he had ever seen.

When the commander touched the young soldier and told him who he was, the wounded man let his fingers creep up the commander's sleeve until he touched the stars on his shoulder. When he reached them, he knew that this was indeed his commander in chief, and he reached for his chalkboard and wrote "Semper fidelis," always faithful, which is the motto of the marines. The commander removed the stars from his shoulder and gave them to the enlisted man.

There is a quality in those who have touched the stars and in those who have touched the cross. The only ones equipped to carry the cross are those who have both touched it and been touched by it. When Methodism—and Christianity—has been at its best, it has always insisted on the primacy of Christian experience.

Only those people who carry an unseen reality, the reality of an experience with the Living Christ, can be counted on in times of great spiritual duress. The interesting thing about this experience is that it has to be primary. You cannot inherit it from your family, nor can you assume that it happened just because some religious rite was done for you. Unless you have said yes to Christ in your own life, you cannot assume that you are a Christian.

The Source of Christian Power

The Council looked at Peter and John and wondered at them with amazement. If we would make the world wonder again, we must insist on the primacy of the Christian experience. For the world is waiting to see power in the life of God's people, power which comes only through the abiding presence of the Holy Spirit.

The power of God does not come through church structure. As Albert Outler said, "If we could have done it with structure, the Methodists would have done it a hundred years ago." Indeed, we sometimes see such proliferation of bureaucracy that we wonder what we are going to do about it. In contrast, the power of the early church was rooted in prayer and communion with God through His Spirit.

Some time ago, I was at a church-related conference which went into its second day before anyone bothered to have a prayer. When we finally got around to praying, we used it like crusts on a loaf of bread. And that is too often the function of prayer—we open with it and close with it. In the early church, every time God wanted to send people on His errands, He interrupted their prayers to tell them.

To be a powerful people, Christians must be prayerful people. There is no lack of power. We just may not have turned it on, or there may be an obstruction in the channel. God would not have asked us to disciple the world for Christ unless He had the power supply necessary to do the job.

Not long ago I went by helicopter eighty-seven miles out

into the Gulf of Mexico to tour an oil rig. When we approached it, and I saw that the pilot was going to land on what looked like a trampoline in the middle of the ocean, I didn't let my weight down. But he still put the helicopter down securely, and I started on my tour of the living facilities and then the drilling operation. I saw as they lowered pipes into the sea and then on down into the earth to where the oil was. Everything demonstrated the latest in technology.

But then I saw a workman dropping something down a pipe. It looked like a handkerchief tied on a piece of steel. He lowered it down one pipe and then the next, and I asked what he was doing. My host said, "That little thing is called a rabbit. We learned a long time ago not to put a pipe down into the bowels of the earth without first checking to make sure there is no obstruction."

With all their scientific ingenuity, they had to use such a simple means to be sure there was no obstruction. We have power aplenty, my people. The world is waiting for folks who have been touched by Jesus and who have been empowered by Him. When they see those qualities in us, they will want to come to Jesus too.

Bannok, Montana was the site of the first gold strike in that territory. The lucky men who made that strike had to return to town for more supplies. They swore each other to secrecy, saying, "Don't tell anybody about our treasure." But after they had bought their supplies and started back to their strike, a crowd of people followed their buckboard. The men turned to each other and asked, "Who told? Who let out the secret?" But no one had.

Finally, someone in the crowd following them said, "Do you wonder why we're here? We ain't sure what you found, but from what we see in your faces, we want some of it."

When you find a treasure, the world will want it too, if

157

they see in your faces how wonderful it is. Our task hasn't changed from that of the early Methodist circuit riders in the colonies. When they started, they said, "Our task is to redeem this continent and to spread scriptural holiness all over the land."

When people see it in our faces, they'll follow us right into the kingdom of our God and of His Christ.